Lord You Are Real

A Collection of Inspirational Writings

Paulette Hall

Paulette Hall
2020

Published by Yawn's Publishing
2555 Marietta Hwy, Ste 103
Canton, GA 30114
www.yawnspublishing.com

All Scripture quoted is taken from King James Version

Library of Congress Control Number: 2020910638

ISBN13: 978-1-947773-79-0 paperback
        978-1-947773-80-6 eBook

Printed in the United States

Introduction

Lord You Are Real is a collection of inspirational poems, songs, writings, and prayers that have arisen out of my heart from the One who loves us. The collection began when I surrendered my life to God and His Lordship over thirty-three years ago. It is my intention, not only that others would glean from the treasure that I have found in Jesus Christ, but that they would also search and find their own relationship in Him.

One of the things I enjoy the most about writing is the time set apart to read the Bible, and the discipline of prayer that prepares my heart. To my surprise, most of the poems became a healing tool not only for myself but for others as well. I must confess that after retiring, I knew I had to step out in faith to compile these writings in a book form.

The first poem "Hear Ye!" came about when I was very discouraged. May it bless you as a song of freedom. Note that each writing is in date order, as my journey with the Lord emerged.

Meanwhile another discipline that I had begun during my quiet time was in the visual arts. Drawing, painting, and creating. Being used by the guidance of the Holy Spirit, my art took on a form of its own. Each piece telling a story from the Bible as a conversation between God and myself. He was teaching me His word through a visual form.

In one creative way, I hand-carved and painted God's word on clay hearts, naming them *The Living Hearts Collection*. Through this process, I could see that God was healing and writing His Word in my own heart. It then became clear to me that God desires to do the same for all His children as it is written in His Holy Word.

There are many more writings and works of art that I hope to share with you in the future.

Nevertheless, it is from these disciplines through the scriptures with God, that the poems and creativity have come. Some of the writings are enhanced with scripture; as well as art and pictures from my own personal photo library. May God's message for your life unfold, and may God bless you through His guidance.

Dedicated to the Glory of God the Father
And to The Lord Jesus Christ The Son and Savior of All
Mankind
And to The Holy Spirit Who Reveals God's Word in Us

And in Honor of His Unconditional Love
that no one be lost.
No not one!

And *His hand is stretched out still.*

Acknowledgements

I must gratefully acknowledge the beautiful lives of my parents, family members, friends, pastors, teachers, mentors, missionaries, coworkers, artisans, and even foreigners who, by the goodness and mercy of God in Christ Jesus (The Messiah) have developed the fertile ground in which I have been planted, and from which I have richly grown. Without them I would not be the person that I am today.

Thank you

Contents

Paulette Hall

Hear Ye!

June 2, 1990

Hear ye! Hear ye! Have you heard?
Jesus Christ is The Word!

Harken! Harken! To the call,
Jesus loves you one and all.

So, if you doubt, laugh, and sneer,
Remember ole slew-foot may be near.

Slew-foot; satan, that O sneaky snake,
He's a liar make no mistake.

So, tell that O lair to let you go,
Cause Jesus Christ is the hand you're gonna hold.

Doubt and fear are satan's favorite things,
To keep you locked up is his sneaky snake game.

So, call out to God in Jesus name,
The heavens will rend, and all things will change.

The powers of darkness cannot prevail,
Cause Jesus Christ has the keys to death and hell.

So, call out to God in Jesus name,
The heavens will rend, and all things will change.

Yes! All things will change in Jesus name,
Because Jesus Christ is the name above all names!

Lord You are Real

When I Bowed Down
June 2, 1990

Father, I bow down, and I thank You so much,
For the Bible You wrote is for me to grow up.

So many years I fumbled and failed,
But You Lord Jesus did prevail.

Now, I bow down on my knees, and I ask, seek, and I
pray,
Thank You Dear Lord for Your Word this day.

I bowed on my knees, You came into my heart,
I bowed on my knees with humbleness that would not
depart.

I bowed on my knees and the joy came inside,
You breathed on me, Oh! What a surprise!

I never dreamed I would experience such love,
When I bowed on my knees the compassion flowed from
above.

I always heard that You loved us so,
But now I know that I know that I know!

How do I tell about this Love inside?
O my Love; Dear Jesus, what a pleasant surprise!

When we ask, seek, knock, and pray,
You will manifest Yourself in a real unique way.

I now desire for others to do and know,
To experience Your love, and abundantly grow.

Paulette Hall

So, come Holy Spirit reveal within,
Bring forth a repented heart that was deeply stained with
sin.

---

*The sacrifices of God are a broken spirit: a broken and a
contrite heart, O God, thou wilt not despise.*

Psalm 51:17

*Thy word have I hid in mine heart, that I might not sin
against thee.*

Psalm 119:11

A Dress of Pink, White, And Blue
June 2, 1990

I made a dress of pink, white, and blue,
A dress that would remind me of You.

Blue was the background with flowers of pink and white,
What a beautiful dress. Oh! What a delight!

The blue was the background that reminds me of
Your sky,
And the pink and white flowers of how You died.

The pink and white flowers remind me of You,
For they have four petals tipped with a crimson hue.

Sometimes I sit and wonder at the signs
You send my way,
In Your creation to stop and say,
I love you my child this very day.

So, I made a dress of pink, white, and blue,
Because I desire to surround myself with things that
remind me of You.

You are love, You are true,
The simple things in life, even a dress of pink, white,
and blue.

Paulette Hall

Jesus My Love
June 2, 1990

I desire to be true to You,
For You are my love and my Savior, too.

The love in my heart reels within,
The love in my heart, where does it begin?

The love in my heart saves all from sin,
Alpha, Omega, Beginning, and End.

The Love in my heart is my biggest fan,
The Love in my heart is the Great I Am!

Galatians 2:20

Dear Jesus,
There Is No More Shame
June 2, 1990

Many years ago, yet not so long ago,
You gave me one seed, one seed to grow.

It was only one seed a few weeks old,
And I chose not to let that one seed grow.

Then months passed by, and another seed was planted,
O Lord, how I have taken You for granted!

I knew in my heart I had done wrong right then,
And could not forgive myself for that sin.

My eyes were blinded and there was darkness within,
I was younger back then living in sin.

I asked many times for Your forgiveness,
Not knowing inside You heard all my distresses.

Ten years passed by of living life my way,
Not realizing You were there trying to say.

Look here My daughter,
Look this way.

I would go to church and hear Your word,
But there was a block that seemed so absurd.

Finally, one day, I came to a point of turning,
And You were there, Your heart burning.

I called out to God, and You heard my cry,
Now I have another try.

6

Paulette Hall

I gave You my whole life, and You showed me within,
That You had forgiven me of all that hidden sin.

Now, I am an overcomer with a second chance,
In giving my life to You Lord, I have a new romance.

I love You dear Jesus, there is no more shame!
Because You have given me a brand-new name.

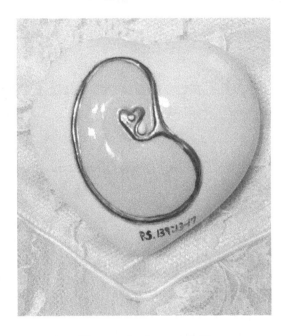

Thou shalt not kill.
Exodus 20:13

*For thou hast possessed my reins: thou hast covered me in
my mother's womb. I will praise thee; for I am fearfully and
wonderfully made: marvelous are thy works; and that my
soul knoweth right well.*
Psalm 139:13-17

. . . thou shalt be called by a new name,
Isaiah 62:2

Lord You are Real

Thank You
June 8, 1990

Thank You Lord, for the peace within,
Thank You Lord, for saving me from all my sin.

Thank You Lord, for Your grace,
Thank You Lord, now I can come face to face.

Personal Experience and Prayer
August 19, 1990

I thank You Father for the tears that gush out of my eyes,
And I thank You Father for the love inside.

Thank You Lord, that You are the light within,
That shines out of me to a world of fallen man.

Purify my heart and burn out all the dross,
For without You Lord I would be lost.

But now I know Your Holy Spirit dwells within,
Because You have chosen me and have made me all new
again.

You said You would send the Comforter, the promise from
the Father through the Son,
And I believe Your Word, and He has come!

So, teach me Holy Spirit the way that I should go.
For my life is a vapor, while I am here, I want to do and
know.

8

Paulette Hall

For when my life is over, the time I lived on this earth,
The things that truly matter are the things of
Your spoken Word.

———————————————

Matthew 4:4, & Matthew 5:16,
John 1:1 & 14, John 1:9, John 1:32-33, John 7:38,
John 14:16-26, John 15:16, II Corinthians 5:17

Spring
April 13, 1992

The birds sing, the flowers bloom, the butterfly flutters,
And my heart is dancing with the "Song" in the air.

It is spring . . . hear O Song of the Lord.

Hear O Song of the Lord
April 15, 1992

The birds sing, the flowers bloom, the butterfly flutters,
And my heart is dancing with the "Song" in the air.

It is spring, hear O Song of the Lord.
It is I who calls, can you see Me? Can you hear Me?
Can you touch Me?

It is I, the Lord who made the heavens and the earth.
Can you see Me? Can you hear Me? Can you touch Me?

It is I who made even you.
Won't you see Me? Won't you hear Me?
Won't you touch Me?

It is I who calls, won't you come?
Won't you come and let Me give you new life?

As the birds do sing, as the flowers bloom,
as the butterfly flutters,
I desire that My Spirit be birthed in you anew.

For the birds, the flowers, the butterflies do what
I created them to do,
But to you I have given choice.

Choose Me this day,
Hear O Song of the Lord.

Paulette Hall

Spring Afternoon
April 16, 1992

I hear Your creation.

Your love is all around me.

Your wind blows across my face, and through my hair.
Your kisses cover me with a veil of joy.

My eyes behold Your beauty.

The flowers dance with bright colors
and do rejoice in the sun.

My ears hear Your creation.
The birds sing praises unto You.
All of nature rejoices in their Maker.

Spring is alive with a "Song"!
Even a butterfly flutters across my path to remind me of
new life in Christ.

My Redeemer! My Maker! My Maker!

Your sun is warm upon my head and back,
Your shade covers my face.

I see an ant scurry across the pavement going about his
Maker's business.

O Maker of my soul, lead me to be about
my Maker's business!

Lord You are Real

A Rendezvous
April 16, 1992

Here we are again, having another lunch rendezvous,
And when there is no one else I can always come to You.

Today is Good Friday, the day the whole world remembers
Your Son Jesus's death,
The price You paid on that Good Friday was
the ultimate test.

Do we really know the pain and tears You suffered?
Are our hearts so hard that they are buffered?

Can we feel Your heartbeat as You hung on the cross?
How can we know the ultimate cost?

Do we dress up in our Sunday's best?
Pleasing God, man, or our self-interest?

Can we not set aside a rendezvous with You?
Speaking sweet, sweet I love Yous?

Moments to escape from the daily routine,
Or are we so busy in our own scheme of things?

Help us to be close to You in prayer and in thought,
And let us not be too busy in our own faults.

To know that You know us each and every one,
And how You long for a rendezvous with Your loved little
ones.

Your love is so grand, Your love is so great,

Paulette Hall

What can we do with all of our mistakes?
Do we put them in a bundle, in a bag, or a box?
Do we sweep them under a rug, or can we just get lost?

No, one cannot hide, no not in a bag or a box,
What does it take? We must go to the cross!

The cross do we yet understand?
How can we know that we are of fallen man?

Our pride, our fine clothes, our eloquent speech,
To the world we can camouflage,
but inside we are naked and weak.

Our sin is before us can we not see,
That we are as filthy as filthy can be.

But thanks be to God for the gift of His grace,
It is His Son; dear Jesus, who cleanses and restores
our faith.

So, take a little rendezvous, a few moments maybe hours,
I will manifest Myself to you with all My hearts desires.

An Old Oak Tree
April 20, 1992

There was an oak tree as big as could be,
But to be cut down was its fate you see.

It stood for years, maybe a hundred or so,
But one day plans were made that it must go.

Construction, streets, and buildings,
Would soon take the place of that old tree's dwellings.

Cut to the ground, cut to the surface,
I ask, what was that old tree's purpose?

Beginning from a seed, asleep in the dirt,
In dew and rain, behold new birth.

The tender limbs grew year after year to be sure,
In the winter, in the spring it continued to endure.

The branches grew tall, the branches grew higher,
Reaching to the heavens was its ultimate desire.

The branches became shade in the long summer days,
Protecting the birds, and animals from the hot sun's rays.

At winter's arrival with arms outstretched,
Mounds of white snow would collect on each branch.

Generations have gone by, still that old tree would stand,
Only now to be cut down by man's own hand.

What was its purpose? What was its plan?
Adoring its Maker and pleasing all men.

As I watched that oak tree being cut limb by limb,

14

Paulette Hall

To be no more I could not grin.

What was its purpose? What was its plan? Maybe to be
painted by an artist's hand,
Or maybe it would inspire a poem or two in the land.

Standing there living seemingly unnoticed in its
beauty and splendor,
To be cut down, oh what an endeavor.

As I watched in sadness I could only frown,
but then with relief,
I could not help but re-think, could my very own life have
been so unique?

To be sturdy, to be strong in all kinds of weather,
Bearing good fruit for many to gather.

The life of that oak tree is now no more,
But the lives that it touched shall forever adore.

Luke 8:15

15

Lord You are Real

New Day
April 21, 1992

As I awake this morn,
Thoughts of You do adorn.

Your Word runs through my heart, and through my veins,
Reeling with joy, what a sweet refrain.

A new day in You filled with laughter, or maybe tears,
No matter what happens, I shall not fear.

You are ever before me, ever so near,
You will never leave me; You tell me I am Your dear.

So much to look forward to this fresh new day,
I wonder who You will bring our way?

I pray for them even now you see,
For I know in my heart that there is a reason we meet.

Paulette Hall

Three Maple Leaves
April 21, 1992

As I entered the doorway at work,
I saw three maple leaves lying on a step unhurt.

The wind must have blown them my way to see,
I took a few glances, maybe two, or three.

What was my heart telling me?
I then knelt down only to see,
is there a message here for me?

Then without hesitation I brought them inside,
To enjoy their presence, what a pleasant surprise!

They would not last long; they would soon wither,
But that did not seem to really matter.

Still intact all three leaves,
I put them on my desk to please.

Three leaves attached to a stem, Alpha, Omega,
Beginning and End,

Reminding me of my Redeemer and Friend!

Prompting
April 21, 1992

I hesitated to write the thoughts in my head,
That someday soon I would be wed.

Would it be possible, could I believe?
Even to extend my family tree?

What are these thoughts, are they childish games?
Or are You prompting my heart for the real thing?

O Holy Spirit, I love You so,
And I want to know, that I know, that I know.

So, until then I will wait,
For You are right on time, and You are never too late.

To be the wife of a godly man,
To be a virtuous woman that is Your plan.

I pray that I will not settle for less,
Than Your very, very, very best!

So, help me be content in my now single life,
And to meditate on Your Word both day and night.

I cannot help but think Lord, if You do not tarry,
You will be this man that I soon will marry.

The marriage supper of the Lamb,
I can hardly wait to hold Your hand.

Prepare Your bride this very hour,
That she be ready for Your ivory tower.

Paulette Hall

Levels of gold, fine jewels, and precious stones,
Will be the place of our new home.

I can hardly wait to see You face to face,
But until then, I will wait.

That Still Small Voice
April 22, 1992

I looked up in the sky to see what was the matter.
Sitting under a shade tree
my spirit seemed to be bothered.

Yet to hear that still small voice deep within,
All seemed so still and silent around me and then...

I looked a little higher, a branch over my head,
There was a robin sitting so pretty and red.

My thoughts were interrupted a few moments or so,
Someone walked by, and we said our hellos.

I looked up again, the quiet robin was gone,
How could I have thought something was wrong?

You were letting me see even though I could not hear,
That still small voice is always near.

In a little bird that was quiet as could be,
On a branch sitting high above little ol' me.

El Roi – The God who sees me

Matthew 6:26
Luke 12:6

Paulette Hall

Arrow of Division
April 23, 1992

Like a flaming sword shot through the air,
There it came, I know not where.

The Mighty Archer with hair so white,
To make a clean heart that is His delight.

The Word of God, the Sword of Love,
Comes swift and straight, lighting like a dove.

The Mighty One looks far and wide,
To find a heart that is humble inside.

He hears the cry within His ear,
The heavens burst open with songs of good cheer.

Mounted on His chariot with one arm in the air,
Shouting through the heavens, I have been waiting for
years!

With fire in His eyes, and the sword of His mouth,
The darkness is absolutely and completely snuffed out.

His flight is so swift; His flight is so sweet,
Coming down by your side, giving immediate relief.

So, when you are in need have no fear,
The cry from your heart He will hear!

Psalms 18

There Is A Stirring
April 24, 1992

Papa, as I share with others the things stirring within,
whether it be in a poem, artwork, or singing a hymn,
Some look at me as if I have gone off the deep end.

I am praising my Heavenly Father with everything I do,
I truly want to please the One and only You.

There is a stirring within I must express,
I cannot hold back what You have addressed!

You have given me talents, talents beyond measure,
Help me to use them for Your good pleasure!

Draw the hearts near that they may see,
It is Jesus who is totally controlling me.

I dare not try to figure out in my head,
The stirring going on in my inner man.

It is Your Holy Spirit that moves and groans within,
Reaching out to sinners that they may be born again.

For You came to give life, You are the life giver,
You gave new life to me, to be a new life teller.

I will shout of You on the mountain tops, and sing of You
in the valleys,

Christ is The Good News!
He is The Grand Finale!

Paulette Hall

Let your light so shine before men,
that they may see your good works,
and glorify your Father which is in heaven.

Matthew 5:16

Lord You are Real

Let's Get Excited
April 24, 1992

I am excited about Jesus, the lover of my soul,
He holds me close in His arms, and never will let me go.

I know I sound dramatic, but I really do not care,
For I know my Lord and Savior,
He is always there.

Yes, I know the Lord and Savior, the lover of my soul,
He has given me a brand-new heart,
and that is the way my story goes.

So, if you say you know the Lord, and you are not excited,
I ask you to look again, you may be undecided.

To waver or to be lukewarm that is a big mistake,
For when you are in the middle it will be much too late.

So, I prompt all to get excited in the things of the Lord,
For He is coming very soon in His mouth a sword.

I do not mean to frighten you, but if I do that is good,
For I am only telling you the things I know I should.

So, let's get excited in the things of the Lord,
God's only begotten Son; dear Jesus,
to be with forevermore.

---

*But ye are a chosen generation, a royal priesthood, an holy
nation, a peculiar people; that ye should shew forth the
praises of him who hath called you out of darkness into his
marvellous light;*
I Peter 2:9

Paulette Hall

Live A Separated Life in Christ
April 25, 1992

To live a life separated,
Seems so strange to those not dedicated.

Dedicated, what is that?
To be in love with the man named Jesus Christ.

To the world we seem so very strange,
They call us fanatics, among other names.

But what can they do? What can they say?
We know Jesus Christ is the only way.

For in our hearts, without a doubt,
We must be completely and totally sold out.

Sold out to Christ is what we must be,
For those who are, the enemy will flee.

Yes, satan will flee from you and me,
By the Blood of Jesus, we are set free.

Under our feet, that is where the enemy will stay,
When we totally surrender and completely obey.

Obey the words of Jesus Christ,
He is the one and only True Light.

He is the righteousness of us all,
And Christ will not let His children fall.

For when we are rooted in the Holy Scriptures,
Nothing can come totally against us.

25

Lord You are Real

Though satan will buffet and do all he can,
To defeat a believer, that is his plan.

So, as we ask, seek, and pray every day,
The Lord Jesus will light the way.

Yes, everyday can be so sweet,
Sold out to Christ we are made complete.

So, live a separated life unto Him,
Others will see, and God will draw them in.

Paulette Hall

The Heat Is On
April 25, 1992

Bask in His presence, and sing a new song,
When the Son shines on you, the heat is on.

The heat is on, the fire from above,
Sent from heaven like unto a dove.

Burning out all the dross,
Purifying and making a brand-new heart.

Lord You are Real

Paulette Hall

Heaven, Your Word, The Sea
April 25, 1992

When I read Your Word, mine eye does see,
Heaven above is like unto Your great sea.

Shall I jump in? Will You rescue me?
For I do not yet understand all that I read.

Yes, I will rescue thee, my precious one,
Come swim in My Word till your days are done.

My Word is like the ocean grand,
With many mysteries yet unknown to man.

Like unto a sea creature deep within the sea,
I have given you gills that you may breathe.

Yes, breathe My Word, the salt water that engulfs
your soul,
It is the Holy Spirit; the gills, which enables you to know.

So, as you swim in the ocean of My Holy Word,
I will reveal the mysteries to you that are not
seen or heard.

For heaven is like unto the Great Sea,
With many mysteries, and treasures that await
you from Me.

---

*The sea is his, and he made it;
and his hands formed the dry land.*

Psalm 95:5

29

Lord You are Real

Salt Shaker Vision
April 26, 1992

My minds-eye saw a salt shaker blown of fine glass,
It had a silver top with small holes to pour out.

Could that salt shaker be a vision from Thee?
To season others as You have seasoned me.

You have refined my head like unto fine silver,
That Your Word go forth in which to deliver.

You have blown Your Word into my soul,
Like unto that salt shaker in which to hold.

God's precious Word that others may know,
It is Your Word, the salt that seasons the soul.

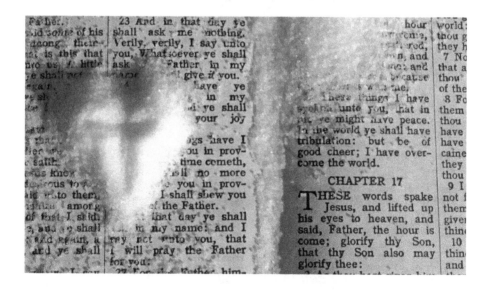

John 17:1-26 & Matthew 5:13-16

Paulette Hall

When Heaven Reached Down, I Looked Up
April 26, 1992

I always thought I wanted to be rich and famous,
But when I found You Lord,
all those thoughts seemed to vanish.

For all the gold in the world, all the fortune and fame,
Can not measure up to Your Holy Name.

Others may wonder and laugh about that,
But it does not really matter,
because I know where my fortune is at.

Nuggets of gold shared from my heart,
Tried by fire never to depart.

Heaven reached down and put within,
Gold nuggets of love so others may live.

When one gives up his own life of gold, fortune, and fame,
To receive God's Most Holy Name.

A gold crown to wear, all will see,
It is heaven above that reached down to thee.

Behold, thou desirest truth in the inward parts: and in the hidden part thou shalt make me know wisdom.

Psalm 51:6

Birth Pains

April 27, 1992

To be an intellectual I am not,
God made the weak things in the world to confound
the wise.

So, I thank You Lord that You made me unique,
No matter what others may think.

For You knew me in my mother's womb,
Fashioned my life that I would bloom.

To bloom into a pretty young lady,
That someday soon I would have my very own babies.

I am single now, no children here of my own,
But there will be many in heaven when I go home.

For there is a burning and turning deep within my belly,
What is this? On the contrary,
I feel like I am actually going to have a baby!

Your Word inside blooms within,
The pains are so real I can hardly hold them in.

So, I ask You Holy Spirit to help me deliver,
Birth forth Your words to bring forth a believer.

---

*The fruit of the righteous is a tree of life; and he that
winneth souls is wise.*

Proverbs 11:30

Paulette Hall

Soap Bar
May 3, 1992

I literally went to wash my hands downstairs
before church service,

And to my surprise, I found the bar of soap there
filthy and dirty.

A popular brand name was engraved on the bar,
But my eyes saw the name Jesus marred like unto
black tar.

Who was the culprit; who dirtied this soap bar?
Must have been satan, the master deceiver from afar.

So, without hesitation, I took the soap bar and ran it
under the water,
The dirt washed away, but only a little.

I had to rub, scrape, and scrub under the running water,
Eventually, that soap bar looked a whole lot better.

You may ask yourself what kind of story is this to be?
But I tell you it really did happen like this to me.

Could this be a lesson for all of us to learn?
That the dirty soap bar represents the church unlearned.

Only with the washing of God's Word daily,
Can the true church be totally liberated.

O how sometimes the soapy water irritates, rubs,
and burns the skin,

But it is needed to wash away all the hidden sin.

33

Lord You are Real

Yet do we come in still with unclean hands?
Polluting one another is satan's very plan.

So, I urge the church to stay under the running water,

Then we will be the true soap bar that we oughta.

Paulette Hall

Time
May 4, 1992

What is time? It clicks away.
Where does it go? I must say!

Time keeps me prompt; it starts my day,
It even lets me know when I am late.

But where does it come from anyway?
The seconds add up to minutes, the minutes add up to
hours, the hours add up to days,

What is this thing called time?

A day is like a thousand years,
and a thousand years are like a day,
Written in the Holy Scriptures,
that is what our Heavenly Father says.

Why have we been given this thing called time?
Do we live this life with no reason or rhyme?

It must be a gift to man, this thing called time,
In keeping a point of measure on a timeline.

Time is a most precious thing!
But where did it come from, where did it begin?

God spoke into existence the heavens and the earth,
For His good pleasure was time's purpose!

To bring forth man out of the clay,
God breathed into his nostrils, behold man was made!

We are human clocks given a mind of our own,

Lord You are Real

And given a heartbeat that clicks seemingly unknown.

With man's own ear there is apparently no sound,
But I ask how is this human clock wound?

This gift of time is like unto a heartbeat,
With every breath there is life to be.

The Divine Watchmaker from above looks down,
To see if there be a seeking heart to be found.

He seems to allow our lives to click away,
No matter what we do or say.

Will these human clocks someday give way?
Will we continue the heartbeat whether or not we stray?

Or is it the choice we make each and every day?

What must one do to find the key?
To be wound from on high for eternity.

The still small voice within me speaks,
It is heaven above that one must seek.

The key to this clock I must find!
But where do I begin this search of mine?

On a hill far away in a segment of time,
With arms outstretched, we were on His mind.

The Key was made at the cross,
Love so divine for all the lost!

The sacrificed Lamb on that hill far away,
Bought the Key to life for all today!

Paulette Hall

Generations have gone by since the Key was wrought,

And time clicks, clicks, clicks away with hardly a thought.

Click, click, click, click, click, click, click, click, click. . .

The time is close at hand for Jesus to return!

Click, click, click!

The Field of Lilies
May 5, 1992

If I could purchase a field for you,
I would purchase a field of lilies.

If I could sing a song for you,
I would sing of the field of lilies.

If I could write a poem for you,
I would write of the field of lilies.

If could paint a picture for you,
I would paint a field of lilies.

Yes, I have done all these things for you
My precious dear,

For when My Son said *"It is finished"*,
was all for you to hear.

The purchase was paid!
The song was sung!
The poem was written!
The picture was painted!

Just for you! For you, My dear, are one of My flowers,
Hand-picked for My field of lilies.

John 19:30

Paulette Hall

The Plumb Line
May 19, 1992

Lord You are the plumb line, the builder of my heart,
The carpenter who works on and repairs
the broken parts.

Your Word is the weight that holds my life straight,
Straight like unto the cord attached to the weight.

An exact vertical work the plumb line measures,
For a building upright, enduring all weather.

You may build me as unto a great ship that travels
over the seas,
Or maybe like unto a house that shelters others in need.

You are the master builder, the plumb line of my heart,
Restoring this old dwelling, each and every part.

The Bible is the blueprint that guides this heart of mine,
For the mighty carpenter builds with His hand so divine.

I cannot help but wonder when
You lived Your life on this earth,
You were the son of a carpenter reflecting
Your Father's work.

Now You are seated at the right hand of God,
Overseeing the construction, waiting for His nod.

For when the restoration is finally completed,
The trump of God will sound for those who are obedient.

Obedient to hear, and see the Master's hand,
Which holds the plumb line on the other end.

A Rainbow Day
May 20, 1992

I asked the Lord to give me a poem for you today,
That your path be a rainbow, coloring your way!

A Lighthouse Tower
May 20, 1992

If I were a ship, I would travel the oceans wide,
Though storm and fog will come,
You are forever at my side.

No matter if this ship of mine be tossed about the seas,
The waves obey Your voice; a calmness comes over me.

Why should I fear the storms in this present life?
For You are *the way, the truth, and the life!*

The Light shining through the darkness over the seas,
Like unto a lighthouse tower, beckoning to ease.

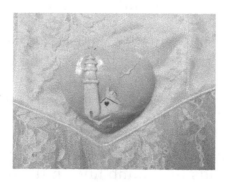

Paulette Hall

Foundations
May 20, 1992

I went to build my house not realizing
the foundation was sand,
Living my life my own way was not the Master's plan.

For when the rains, floods, and winds beat
upon this house,
The foundation began to shift and sink;
disaster was all about.

Finally realizing the error of my wicked way,
Was not listening or hearing
Your voice telling me I must obey.

I then cried out for help, to heaven above,
A rock came forth beneath my feet breaking through
the sand and slug.

Lifting me above the ground, the rock about my feet,
Molding quick, hard, and fast, like unto concrete.

No longer to stand on the shifting sand,
this house became complete.

For when you are on the Rock of Jesus Christ,
satan cannot defeat.

Idols
May 20, 1992

To be a baseball player I am not athletically inclined,
But to be a brave prayer warrior on God's battle lines.

Basketball to the world is a most exciting sport,
Many go there seeking excitement on the court.

Golf a quiet and unusual game,
To putt or drive a small ball across a green.

Tennis could become a menace to man's mind,
Blocking God's love will keep man blind.

Football, another sport for man to indulge,
Pays high wages, and the subtle deception goes on.

Boxing O what a brutal thing,
To be punched out before the final ring.

Horse racing, gambling, the gate becomes wider,
Hollywood, movies, videos, TV, and race car drivers.

Is man looking to man to fill his every dream?
What is man truly seeking,
wrapped up in all these things?

Money, fine cars, boats, electronics,
and things, things, things,
Take up man's time and blocks out the real thing!

Ads, commercials, news, sitcoms, billboards, magazines,
and junk food books,
The deception goes on; man seems to be hooked.

Paulette Hall

Drugs, violence, pornography, alcohol, and abuse,
all are sin,
The gate becomes wider, many go therein.

Money, money, money, things, things, things,
Idols, they have become gods, with counterfeit names.

No longer for grown-ups, the deception reaches lower,
To the little children, we are raising
a generation of evildoers.

The corporate world stresses man to be self-sufficient,
Relying on self to be totally dependent.

A lie from satan, the work of self,
One can-do no-good thing without God's help.

The world says believe in anything you wish,
Now religion has become just another click.

Many have itching ears to hear what they want,
Because man's lifestyle has become
misled and morally broke.

The Word of God says, *for wide is the gate, and broad is
the way that leadeth to destruction,*
And man keeps living in the fast lane blinded
from God's direction.

Man keeps looking to sin to fill all his dreams,
And satan is the culprit, peddling all the schemes.

Many have become pawns at satan's very hand,
To deceive many, many a man.

The gateway to hell grows wider, and wider,
Man is caught in a web, and satan is the spider.

Lord You are Real

Can man not see that he is going on a downhill spiral?
That leads to death cut off from God's power.

To turn from every evil way, man's journey begins at the
straight and narrow gate,
For if you do not turn from sin, it will be much too late.

The Word of God is there for all to find the narrow way,
God will teach you by His Holy Spirit this very day!

The carnal mind cannot understand the things of
the Holy Spirit,
So, repent from your sins, ask Jesus to come in,
then your ear will hear Him.

Blind eyes will open for you will see,
It is God above that loves you and me.

The walk is sweet at the narrow gate,
A new beginning of Love that the world absolutely hates.

The cost will be great as you enter therein,
Many will laugh who you thought were your friends.

The treasures you will find will be worth it all,
Because you are now a believer with a new life cause.

So, tell the world of Jesus, your newfound friend,
They were like you, deceived in their own sin.

Matthew 7:13
I Timothy 6:10
II Timothy 3:1-9

Paulette Hall

May the Rains Come
May 22, 1992

The day is here in 1992,
The powers of darkness could be controlling you.

Good is said to be evil, and evil is said to be good,
Woe unto this generation, they know not what they do.

Man's spirit has become like unto a dry ground,
No water or rain seems to be found.

The fragmented pieces within man's heart,
Are dry, brittle, and cracked like unto a desert parched.

Man needs a great rain that will flood his soul,
To make the fragmented pieces in his heart whole.

This drought of man's heart has been taking its course,
But now it is time for the clouds to break forth.

Prayer warriors; the intercessors of God,
stand on the front lines,
Praying for the lost that none would be left behind.

Many are blinded and trapped by satan's lies,
But prayer warriors are standing
in the gap for those very lives.

The Great Intercessor; Jesus Christ,
God's only begotten Son,
Holds His scepter high,
for there are many souls to be won.

To have life eternal with God above,
That is His purpose, His purpose of Love.

Lord You are Real

The war rages on, the evil against the good,
But the end of the book says satan is doomed!

So, wave your banners high, and march on through,
The rain is coming, it is coming very soon!

Revival, Revival, Revival in the land,
This is our prayer, praying for all men!

So, saints of God pray, and march on through,
Be diligent in prayer this 1992!

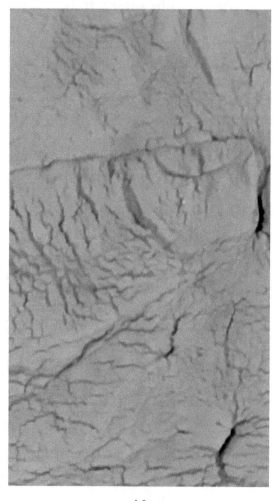

Paulette Hall

Butterfly Song
June 1, 1992

If I could be a butterfly, I would ride with you to work,

I would dance and prance around your head
and sing you songs of worth.

Worthy, Worthy, Worthy, Worthy is the Lord!
Holy! Holy! Holy! Holy is the Lord!

This butterfly was once a worm inching along life's way,

But now a new creature in Christ
with a song of worth to say.

Worthy, Worthy, Worthy, Worthy is the Lord!
Holy! Holy! Holy! Holy is the Lord!

Philippians 4:8

Lord You are Real

YOU ARE
June 1, 1992

For you Are! You Are! You Are!

You are **A**dored! You are **R**everenced! You are **E**verlasting!

You **A R E** my forever King! ! !

Hidden Wounds
June 8, 1992

The hidden wounds of the heart man cannot see,
It is God alone who looks within thee.

He sees the bruised places, the hurts inside,
And longs to heal when we let Him abide.

I have loved thee with an everlasting love: therefore with lovingkindness have I drawn thee.

Jeremiah 31:3

48

Paulette Hall

A Song for a Friend
June 21, 1992

May our Lord and Savior bloom within,
That your life would be a fragrance
that would draw all men unto Him.

My prayer and song for a friend.

II Corinthians 5:15

Bloom
June 21, 1992

May the Word of God bloom within,
That your life would be a fragrance
that would
draw all men unto Him.

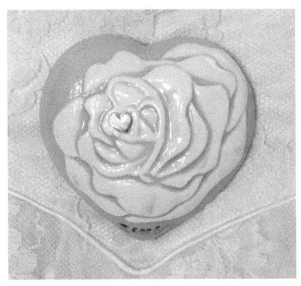

Purple Passion
June 21, 1992

I saw a plant the other day,
It caught my eye, so I looked that way.

So strange to see a purple glow,
I got up a little closer you know.
The leaves were green but there was a purple glow?

The closer I got to the plant I could see,
It had a fuzz of purple upon its leaves.

So fine, so delicate, so soft and sweet,
A purple glow of passion, oh so unique.

Could my life be as the plant I saw?
Being close to my Savior reflecting a purple glow?

A glow of compassion upon my skin,
Reflecting the love of Jesus from deep within.

---

*I am the vine, ye are the branches: He that abideth in me,
and I in him, the same bringeth forth much fruit: for
without me ye can do nothing.*

John 15:5

50

Paulette Hall

It's Raining Inside
June 25, 1992

Rainbows come and rainbows go,
Without the rain they never show.

So, if you see a tear upon my cheek,
You have made a rainbow inside oh so unique!

A New Day
June 26, 1992

A morning yawn, with a stretch or two,
My head still groggy, do I have to get up this early?

My flesh is weak, but The Spirit is willing,
To spend a moment with You can be so revealing.

My flesh says I do not have time, what must I do?
This bed of mine is oh so cozy and um-m-m-m!

Your Spirit inside says it's a new day,
The flesh is weak and wants to stay.

As this flesh gets up Your Spirit rises,
A new day in Christ full of fantastic surprises!

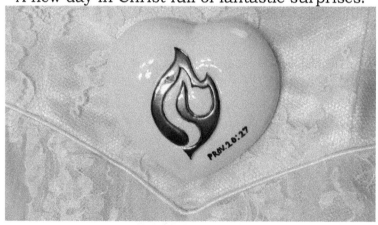

*Watch and pray, that ye enter not into temptation: the
spirit indeed is willing, but the flesh is weak.*
Matthew 26:41

*The spirit of man is the candle of the Lord, searching all
the inward parts of the belly.*
Proverbs 20:27

Paulette Hall

Bedtime
June 26, 1992

As I lay me down to sleep,
Mine arms clasp around Your Word to keep.

To rest in my Lord my heart does yearn,
Sweet dreams do appear from a heart that is learned.

Your Word held tight unto my chest,
With thoughts of You Lord, I am happy and blessed!

*It is written, Man shall not live by bread alone, but by
every word that proceedeth out of the mouth of God.*
Matthew 4:4

Sanctify them through thy truth: thy word is truth
John 17:17

A New Song in My Heart
July 21, 1992

Sing O daughter of Zion; shout, O Israel;
be glad and rejoice with all the heart,
O daughter of Jerusalem. Zephaniah 3:14

Sing! Sing! Sing the Song of God!
Sign! Sing! Sing the Song of God!

Jesus is the Song within my heart,
The note that plays the key.

Jesus is the Song within my heart,
That raptures you and me.

So, play me O Lord,
Play me O Lord.

The Song of God within my heart is Jesus!

Play the note within my heart,
Play the note of God.

Play the note within my heart The Song of God,
The Song of God.

Jesus is The Song,
Jesus is The Song!

Paulette Hall

Bouquet of Love
September 1, 1992

If I could be an instrument in God's own hand,
I would be like unto a piano with strings so grand.

To play you a birthday song, a song of love,
Where tulips and daisies burst forth from above.

To perfume the air with compassion and love,
From the One who loves you, God's only begotten Son.

May rainbow flowers fill your heart today,
A bouquet of divine love sent your way.

Lord You are Real

On A Cloudy day
September 4, 1992

Father, it looks like rain; the sky is overcast,
No matter how dreary a day, with You life is truly a blast!

The sunshine is hidden; it is gray all around,
My heart grows heavy with the clouds that abound.

Never will I fear, because You are ever so near,
Near to a heart that is very, very dear.

Yes, the sun is hidden in the clouds above,
Yet the Son shines within, His unconditional love!

Paulette Hall

Fall
October 21, 1992

Fall is in the air . . . leaves falling all around,
One leaf spins here, another drifts to the ground.

With the sound of rustling papers,
the leaves drag the blacktop surface,
Then another one somersaults across;
what is its purpose?

What is this meaning of fall? My mind does ponder,
Seeing Your wind blow, I wonder and wonder!

The sap is leaving the branches
preparing for winter's sleep,
O take not Thy Holy Spirit from me,
may He keep, keep, keep!

Is fall a season of life? Yes, how well I should know . . .
A time of stillness, of rest,
and ask is all well with my soul?

Yes, a time to be still and know that You are God,
Another year almost over, desiring the Father's nod.

A year of service to You, my Lord, have we done well?
That is my desire to hear; only time will tell.

To stand for what is good, I will stand with my Friend,
For You are my Redeemer, to the very end!

*To every thing there is a season, and a time to every
purpose under the heaven: ...*

Ecclesiastes 3:1-8

57

Lord You are Real

Longing for That City
October 26, 1992

My heart longs for a country . . . that City!
A place mine eye has never seen.

It is called the New Jerusalem,
Beyond the Crystal Sea.

There will be streets of gold,
No, it will not be the yellow-brick road.

The real thing it will be,
For all eternity!

Levels of precious stones,
With the names of God's chosen ones.

For I long for that City, mine eye has never seen,
A place that shines of Light, from the Almighty King!

Paulette Hall

Fashion This Clay
November 9, 1992

My heart does quake within me.
How broken and undone that I am.

Thinking I am something I am not. Help me!
Standing before You, my Lord,
You see every flaw, every sin.

No thought of my own is of any significance.
Clothe me now with Your love,
clothe me now with Your grace.

For I am naked and bare in heart
before my Lord and King.

Dear God, save this wretched soul that I am,
For You alone are Holy!

May Your perfection come forth in my life,
For my very life would not exist without You.

For You made me, and You know me.
Remove the spots, and smooth out the wrinkles.

May this vessel be ready and dressed,
for the coming of our Lord and Savior Jesus Christ.

Oh, how precious is the blood that was shed for All!

Proverbs 3:5-6 & Isaiah 64:8

59

One Life Lived
March 3, 1993

I lived one life, one life on this earth,
It was a good life, now I am in heaven full of
joy and mirth.

If I could be an instrument for you now in
God's own hand,
I would be like unto a majestic organ with cords so grand.

I would play you a song, a song of love,
Where tulips and daisies burst forth from above.

To perfume the air with compassion and love,
From the One who loves you, God's only begotten Son.

So, may rainbow flowers fill your heart today,
A bouquet of Divine Love sent your way.

Now close your eyes! See the notes dancing
through the air,
Mingled with soft rose petals falling against your hair.

Yes! Kisses and hearts are floating all around your face,
Reminding you of our Lord's Glory and
His Amazing Grace.

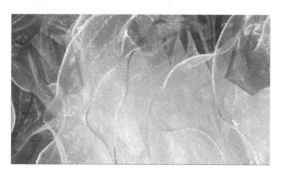

60

Paulette Hall

Life's Ebb and Flow
April 5, 1993

Like an ocean wave with peak so high,
The foam rolls in with no reason why.

A mighty force, yet so serene,
A mystery the ocean waves do bring.

One life to live, one never knows,
The paths we will cross with life's ebb and flow.

Rhapsody in Bloom
April 5, 1993

The Song of the ages in purple Majesty,
Rings true in a heart of red, white, and blue.

Red for the blood that was shed for all men,
White for the cleansing of all the hidden sin,
Blue for the wounds, setting the captives free.

Rhapsody in bloom came forth for you and me.
Rhapsody in bloom shed at the cross,

The Song of Divine Love for all the lost.

Paulette Hall

Changing of The Guard
April 5, 1993

The trumpets do sound, the guard standing at the gate,
A mighty sound the trumpeters do make.

A call to arms, raising their banners high,
The Lord of all is waiting for His bride,

Blow ye the trumpets, the trumpeters of the Lord,
The time is drawing nigh at hand
for the changing of the guard.

We will usher in the King of kings, the Mighty One of God,
Give ear ye chosen seed before the changing of the guard.

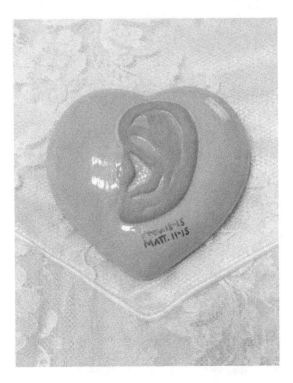

To Be A Flower
April 13, 1993

If I could be a flower, I would smell of fragrance fresh,
I would bend and sway within the breeze displaying
my Father's best.

Adorned with colors divine,
Reflecting the bright Son-shine.

A flower I would be for all the world would see,
The beauty of my Maker who designed and fashioned me.

Paulette Hall

Quiet
April 24, 1993

Your Word rests upon my chest,
A quiet peace of pure rest.

To guide my soul this very day,
New steps we will take along the way.

An adventure You and I will be,
Your hand in mine for many will see.

The walk by faith, not by sight,
For I am Yours and all is right.

Your peace will be my countenance for sure,
The love within forever will endure.

Take not Thy Holy Spirit from me this day,
For I ask, seek, and pray.

Hand-in-hand My love, we will go,
To places that forever unfold.

A love that man has never seen,
To dwell with the forever King!

A fragrance of cinnamon and spice,
The fruit of the Spirit is oh so nice.

So peace be still; the waters are calm,
Walk by faith till the day is dawn.

*Now faith is the substance of things hoped for,
the evidence of things not seen.*

Hebrews 11:1

When Love Overflowed
May 10, 1993

My heart is moved; what could this be,
Tears well up, could someone here love me?

Yes, You love me Lord; that is true,
But are You sending me someone for me to love, too?

My heart is in wonder; my heart is in hope,
To let down my guard, help me to cope.

Let not my heart be hurt again,
But if it be, You will always be my friend.

For You sent Your Son, the lover of my soul,
He will keep my heart; for it was foretold.

In a time, in a place, only God knows,
The Maker of the heart when love overflowed.

Jesus wept. John 11:35
Immanuel … God with us.

Paulette Hall

Rivers of Living Water
May 11. 1993

Rivers of living water, You are my oasis,
Rivers of living water, flow from Your graces.

Rivers of living water, give my soul rest,
Rivers of living water, I know I am happy and blessed.

Rivers of living water, I hear the sound of it,
Rivers of living water, from Your Holy Spirit.

Rivers of living water, that mighty rushing wind,
Rivers of living water, washing away all sin.

Rivers of living water, my soul longs for,
Rivers of living water, from Your throne pour.

Rivers of living water, I shall never thirst again,
Rivers of living water are from the Great I Am!

John 4:14 & John 7:37

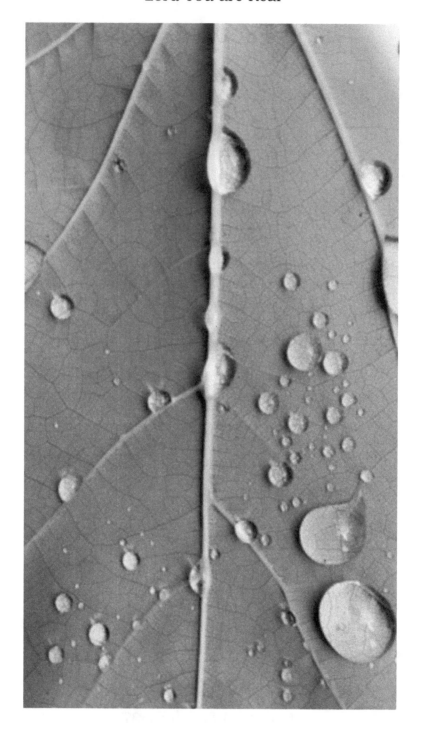

Paulette Hall

Tears
July 23, 1993

Tears are a most precious thing,
They wash and cleanse like a springtime rain.

Do not be ashamed of the tears you see,
They are tears indeed from the Almighty King!

For I died for you, and I cried for you,
The precious dewdrops a new morning spring.

So, do not fret when the waters flow,
They are from My Heart raining a soft white snow.

Cool and refreshing the chill is sweet,
My love for you I would repeat.

To lighten your heart, to let you know,
I am washing and cleansing with the new fallen snow.

It only took one broken heart,
He died and wept to give you a new start.

The tears were spilled and overflowed,
a sign to let creation know,
I am the water that makes one grow.

Yes, the water fills the broken gaps,
To seal the heart and keep it intact.

So, without the tears there is no pain,
And without the pain there is no gain.

Isaiah 55:10-13

69

As We Come to You
August 2, 1993

O Papa! Do we come to You one way, then go another?
Let us seek Your face, that we will truly discover.

You are the helper of our hearts,
to be sure and true to You,
Steadfast in Your love,
Your Word teaches us what to say and do,

So, let us not seek our own will or way,
But let us seek Your face each and every day.

For Your Word transforms and heals within,
You created man to be born again.

Open blind eyes to see that we are nothing on our own,
God above You are, You are seated on Your throne.

Paulette Hall

Trust Me
August 23, 1993

Why ask why? Trust in Me.

When you cannot see the way, I make the way!
I am the Way Maker!
Trust Me! Trust Me!

Happy are those who know the God of Jacob.
Who have their minds set.

Water blossoms and cherries are sweet to the taste,
Like unto My Word, a spray of Glory and Grace.

A sweet fragrance mingled with passion and love,
A bouquet of red roses sent from above.

When there is no one to send you flowers,
I do.

When there is no one to hug you,
I do.

When there is no one to kiss you,
I do.

You are My bride, and I long to love you like no other.
You are My bride!

To Come Away with You!

September 2, 1993

To come away with You.
To steal away with You.
There is none other like You.

Be still and know that "I Am".
I am the Alpha, the Omega,
The First and the Last!
The soon coming King!

Your banqueting table!
The Feast of Tabernacles.
Show me O Lord what this is?
The Feast of Tabernacles?
What is this Lord?
What is this?

The Marriage Supper of The Lamb

Paulette Hall

You Are Beauty
October 8, 1993

If words could describe your beauty,
I would sing a song to you.

Wrapped in bows and yellow daffodils,
I would sing a song for you.

Happy birthday to My daughter; your beauty is refined,

Like threads of silver and gold you are Mine, you are
Mine, you are Mine!

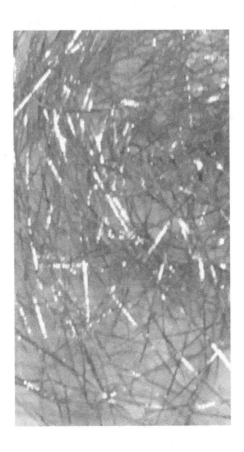

Lord You are Real

An Adventure to Israel
November 8, 1993

As I gaze out the window Your glory I see,
Gold and yellow leaves, truly You are with me!

Autumn, the trees are laughing with colors
of soon winter's sleep,
I love Your name Dear Jesus; You adore and keep.

You will keep me in Your watchful care
though winters may come,
Your Son will keep me warm
till all my days here are done.

O Papa! Papa! Lover of my soul.
I long for that country mine eye cannot see,

You have impressed a longing, yearning deep within me.

Thank You for the crimson, yes,
the stone was rolled away,

I am with you here My daughter,
always here to stay.

For you are away with Me, away with Me this day,
An adventure of a lifetime, you chose to come away.

_____

II Corinthians 5:15

74

Paulette Hall

The Stone and The Rock
November 11, 1993

The stone that was rolled away was only a pebble
compared to the Rock of Ages inside the tomb.

Isaiah 28:16-17

Laughter in Israel
November 14, 1993

Thank You for laughter Lord!

For allowing me to enjoy Your Land.

To be as a little child.

Kissing Your Land with my feet.

To see Your beauty as we walk.

To come away with my King!

---

*Now therefore ye are no more strangers and foreigners, but
fellow citizens with the saints, and of the household of
God. And are built upon the foundation of the apostles and
prophets, Jesus Christ himself being the chief corner stone;*

Ephesians 2:19-20

Lord You are Real

To Be Desired
January 29, 1994

Just like we as humans desire to be loved . . .
You Lord must desire to be loved too!

Lord, how Your very own heart must long,
yearn and desire to be loved.
You desire to be touched,

You desire to be seen,
You desire to be wanted,

You desire to be thought of often,
You desire to be conversed with,

You desire to be held,
You desire to be hugged,

You desire to be needed,
You desire to be longed for,

You desire to be respected,
You desire to be looked upon with adoration,

You desire to be loved,
You desire to be kissed.

You desire our love, those
You have created.

You desire me Lord,
You desire me,

You desire my love!

Paulette Hall

Golden Threads
April 23, 1994

There will be threads left.

As you go and do.

There will be threads left.

Threads of hope.

Threads of Me.

Threads of rejoicing in Me.

As you go and do.

Go and do.

There will be threads left.

Threads of Me.

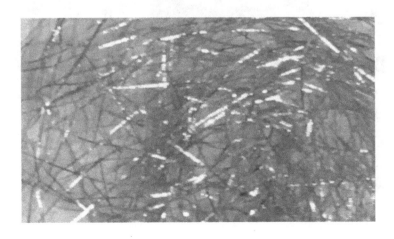

Heart Strings
May 15, 1994

Play our heart strings, O Lord.

That perfect praise and adoration be made known unto You.

Play our heart strings, O Lord.

A perfect song to our God.

Play our heart strings again and again.

That we may revel in Your Love.

Play our heart strings, O Lord!

Paulette Hall

Two Paths Crossed
September 2, 1994

Seasons come and seasons go,
Change is all around.

People come and people go,
But which way do they go?

If by chance in our meeting, a glimpse of heaven you see,
The eye an open door to the soul.

The reason being the eye to my heart,
Is the Savior who made me whole.

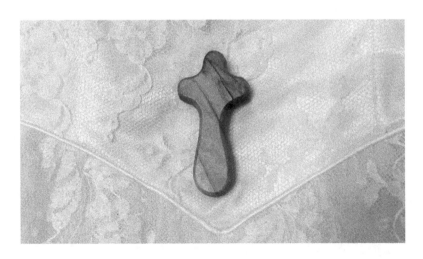

*The light of the body is the eye: if therefore thine eye be
single, thy whole body shall be full of light.*

Matthew 6:22

The Wondrous Story
September 2, 1994

If I could tell the story, I'd preach it far and wide,
I'd raise my voice a hearken, awakening those that hide.

I'd preach the glorious gospel, the mighty rejoicing sound,
I'd tell the wondrous story to those that would be found.

My feet would be a shaking,
I'd preach till my breath was gone,
My soul would be a quaking, the voice inside is the Song.

Tell! Tell! Tell! Oh!

The Wondrous Story!

Paulette Hall

Like unto A Sea Breeze
September 3, 1994

Sea breeze, sea breeze where do you come from?
Sea breeze, sea breeze a mystery known only to God.

Sea breeze, sea breeze fragrance is all around,
Sea breeze, sea breeze my heart does abound.

Sea breeze, sea breeze radiant rhapsody,
Sea breeze, sea breeze born for eternity.

Sea breeze, sea breeze the Holy Spirit brings,
Sea breeze, sea breeze a new and wonderful thing.

Sea breeze, sea breeze where did you come from?
Sea breeze, sea breeze blown in from heaven above.

Sea breeze, sea breeze a wonderful thing,
Sea breeze, sea breeze melts my heart to sing.

Sea breeze, sea breeze so soft, refreshing, and sweet,
Sea breeze, sea breeze no more reason to hate.

Sea breeze, sea breeze a love so true and pure,
Sea breeze, sea breeze forever to endure.

Sea breeze, sea breeze blow on every face,
Sea breeze, sea breeze man to receive
Your Glory and Grace.

Sea breeze, sea breeze make Your presence known,
Sea breeze, sea breeze prepare us for our new home.

Sea breeze, sea breeze strengthen man's heart,
Sea breeze, sea breeze never to depart.

Lord You are Real

Sea breeze, sea breeze a rush from heaven above,
Sea breeze, sea breeze kindling a new love.

See breeze, see breeze, I do see! I do see!
The breath from heaven above is Thee!

Paulette Hall

Owed to A Friend
September 6, 1994

So many things left unsaid,
Days pass by mounting dread.

Time slips away; the past left behind,
Few words spoken left in time.

A chosen word rekindles the heart.
What must I say, where do I start?

Few words spoken left unsaid,
A chosen word spoken; I forgive.

Lord You are Real

Nail Scarred Hands
September 12, 1994

Where do I begin in the recesses of my mind?
To call upon the name of the Most High.

Thank You Lord, for this quiet little place,
Thank You Lord, Your arms do embrace.

New beginnings from ashes of old,
A new life in You the pages unfold.

Redeemed! Restored by the blood of the Lamb,
A surprise each day when holding Your hand.

Treasures sought after yet hidden within,
Reveal the kingdom of heaven touched by
the Nail-Scarred Hands.

Paulette Hall

My Heart
September 12, 1994

Music, a melody from the heart.
The Song of Divine Love. My Heart! My Heart!

Like unto A Swing
September 16, 1994

Emotions are a funny thing,
High and low like unto a swing.

One foot on the ground, two feet and stop,
A stub of the toe, then go flop.

Regain my sight looking above from the dirt,
Holding the foot, O how it hurts.

The Son is shining down, a wonderful thing,
O how I love to swing with my King.

With His thumb and finger holding the rope,
The Savior above is our only hope.

Therefore, I will sit in His swing on high,
For I trust in the Lord as He draws me nigh.

Peaceful Sound
September 16, 1994

The passing of a willows will,
A peaceful sound, heart be still.

Weeping may endure for a night, but joy cometh in the morning.

Psalm 30:5

Paulette Hall

Echoes of Love
September 16, 1994

My heart sings unto thee jubilant adoration.
Jubilant echoes, echoes of Love.

Rippling through time and space.
Echoes of Love! Echoes of Love!

Lord, You are my Love! Sing on my heart! Sing on!
The Song has been sung. Echoes of Love!

Lord, Your heart is beating! A love Song!
Your heart is beating! Echoes of Love!

Jesus in my heart! Echoes of Love!
Vibrant melody! Jubilant adoration unto Thee!

Sing on! Sing on!
Exalting **C**hrist **H**ummed **O**n **E**ternal **S**trings,
Omnipotent **F**ire,
Lead **O**n **V**irtuous **E**ncounter.

Radiant Rhapsody!
Exalting **C**hrist **H**ummed **O**n **E**ternal **S**trings!

Strands of Golden Love, Grace echoes from within,
The Song! The Song! The Song has been sung!

O heart of mine, peace so divine!
Play me O Lord! Play the Song!

Radiant Rhapsody! Echoes of Love!

Thoughts of You
September 27, 1994

Walking down a path one day,
Cover me Lord, this I pray.

Looked down on the ground, an acorn did see,
Picked it up, so strange to me.

The cap of the acorn covered the hull,
A tiny part showed only a nub.

You were talking to me in my thoughts as we walked,
You have covered me Lord as the acorn picked up.

Psalm 91

Psalm 36:7

Paulette Hall

Precious Anointing
September 30, 1994

My heart spins within, a love with no lack,
Let me express this Love, hold me not back.

My cup runs over; I cannot contain the flow,
What a wonderful Love, this I know.

Iridescent jewels flow upon my head and neck,
From Your throne of grace, You keep me in check.

Your anointing, Your anointing!
Precious anointing from above,

Your holy oil, sweet melody! A fragrance of Your Love!

Lord You are Real

To Be and To Know
September 30, 1994

To be,
Is to be in Your presence.

To know,
Is to rest in Your love.

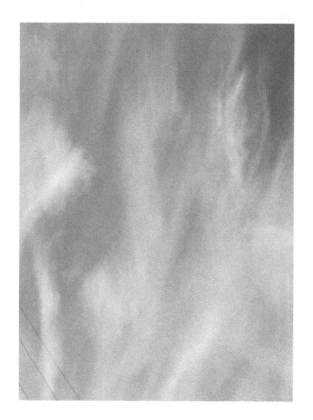

Be still, and know that I am God:

Psalm 46:10

Paulette Hall

Romancing the King
January 6, 1995

Dear Lord,

It is a new year. I wait. As I sit with pillows behind my
back resting in front of a warm cozy fire,
my heart and mind ponder Your serenity.

With knees propped up; they are much warmer than my
face. I guess because they are much closer to the fire.

I hear the flapping of the flames and crackling of the
wood. My eyelids are hot. I see the colors of the kindling
fire; blue, white glowing orange timbers.

My brow has become hot, my forehead absorbs the heat.
The fire is quieting down now; much of the wood has
collapsed in piles of glowing dust.

White smoke flows upward on one side. It is time to put
another log on the fire.

Tinkling sounds whisper as the new log begins to take
hold of the remaining flames.

The fire is hotter; blue colors appear. A burst of airy
sound takes hold as the new log is engulfed.

The heat is intense. Only the right side of the log is
consumed. The other side awaits for the flames to climb
over. Quiet . . . still . . . then a flash of new heat!
A glorious celebration arises!

The left side rejoices in the laughter of the joining in.
The singing of a symphony. Then a log collapses as

91

Lord You are Real

the others beneath give way. The heat rises to an
intense roaring robust flame.

Lord, may Your people lay their all on Your altar.
To burn for You! Let not the fire go out!

Rejuvenate the sound.
Quietly burn away the dross.

Simmer Your people to glow and radiate for You.
The smell of the wood is sweet!

The burning timbers give off a fragrant aroma of their
own.
It is time to put another log on the fire.

I see with mine eyes the new roaring flame.
The fire is hotter than it ever was. Intense.

In Love! I hear the wood sizzle where the sap is wet.
Then a loud pop.

The flames clap and laugh as the glowing timbers burn.
A rejoicing has taken place.
It is time to put another log on the fire.

A continuous burning Your love is! A continuous burning!
"Rejoice with Your God. Rejoice in the dance.
Clap your hands, and rejoice, and again I say rejoice!"

Thank You for Your fire Lord. You are the all-consuming
fire! *Lift up your heads, O ye gates;
and be ye lift up, ye everlasting doors; and the King of
glory shall come in.* Psalm 24:7

A log drops, the coals ignite. A fervent heat releases into
the air. . . then a resting . . . the flames sound like they

Paulette Hall

are breathing. Listen!

Breathe on us, O Lord.
May we Your people be listening
and in tune to hear Your voice!
Thank You for speaking O Lord!

A piece of wood moves. . . an adjustment is made.
The timbers whistle in new fervency . . . a higher
temperature is claimed . . . then a resting . . . quiet gasps,
and gentle puffs go up. A crackling . . . a drop of coal and
ash . . . a simmering . . . a gentle rest. A warm caress of
Your love hugs each burning log . . . they are glowing!
Your glory is all around those who burn for You.

Thank You Lord, for speaking while I enjoyed
a cozy fire in my fireplace at home.

You are my fireplace!
Within whispers Your warmth . . . a sparkling of
hot love . . . I see sparks flying upward as the last of the
wood shrinks in size and drops
to the top of the accumulated ash.

A mound of hot coal remains . . .
waiting for another log . . .
blow on us, O Lord!

Rekindle the Flame! Let not Your fire go out, and that
Your people stay hot after You!
In Jesus name I pray. Amen.

The Awaiting
January 21, 1995

Just to sit on a grassy knoll with You, Lord. I see Your
wind blowing upon and through Your grass.

The blades laugh with joy as Your rush upon them is
received in expectant awaiting.

And with Your sun touching each slender blade, the
warmth of Your gladness appears
in green shimmers of love.

Your breath flowing over the grassy knoll, a pleasant sight
to the eye. New Life, green and fresh where no man has
walked before. You await a response of gladness from
Your people, O Lord.

A New Touch! A Fresh Breath! A Love Divine! New! New!
New! The Creator hugs His creation in wind, sun, and
rain. Your breath! Your warmth! Your cleansing!

You speak all around Your people. Can we not see?
Can we not hear? Can we not feel?

Take the scales off our eyes to see, to hear, to feel, to
touch, to smell, to taste, and to know You.
Just to know You! You await!

94

Paulette Hall

Heavens Valentine

For God so lo**V**ed the world
That He g**A**ve
His on**L**y
begott**E**n
So**N**
Tha**T** whosoever
Believeth **I**n Him
Should **N**ot perish
But have **E**verlasting life

John 3:16

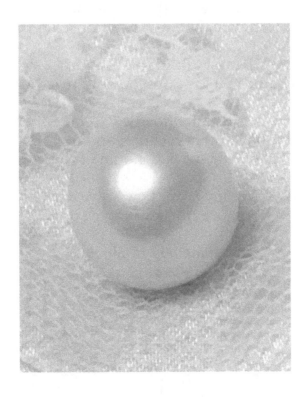

Matthew 13:45-46

Melody in Bloom

January 24, 1995

I just love You Lord! My Valentine!
You have opened Your heart to me.

O Papa, I never dreamed of a love so pure, so sweet,
and so near.

You are close to me. My love for You is real.
My heart is set. Nothing shall separate us!

You have good things for me Lord.
You will complete what you have started.

I trust You Lord. My Lord.
Thank You for our moments together.

A treasure set in time. No one can take them away.
You have them recorded in Your book.
O how great is the sum of them!

My Love, my Love, how I love my Love!
You are my Love Dear Lord.

My melody in bloom!

Paulette Hall

Feet
January 27, 1995

Where will these feet go? Only You know, only You know!
As I stand, I stand for You Lord. I stand for You!
Maker of my soul, I stand!

Feet have five toes each, an arch attached to the heel.
The sole makes up the bottom of the foot,
a reminder our footprints are real.

So, with each step taken, guard them aright,
For great is the path that stands and walks for
Jesus Christ.

So, walk ye in it! Walk ye there!

Walk ye in it with My tender loving care.

Lord You are Real

Mighty Adorned Prince M.A.P.
January 28, 1995

Is my life mapped out to go overseas?
Is my life mapped out to help others in need?

Is my life mapped out to step across the sea?
Is my life mapped out to bring others home with me?

For there is a country mine eye has never seen,
The new awaiting Jerusalem mapped out for you, and me.

The Holy City, a most appealing place,
The M.A.P. of my life stands before my very face.

Paulette Hall

Lily of The Valley
January 28, 1995

All in a day's work, all is planned out.
No matter how we hurt inside, no matter if we shout.

The Lord watches over His children with
tender loving care,
Even though it seems like He is not even there.

For it is not by our feelings that we can know
His presence,
Faith comes by trusting the hand of eternal existence.

So, when you are down and out in a valley oh so deep,
Look for the lily, the smell is oh so sweet.

The Wanderer
January 28, 1995

Why do I wander?
Some days I find myself just wandering.

Looking, taking things in, trying to cover up the
emptiness of being alone,

Wandering, pondering, edging to the surface of
broken unfinished dreams.

Hoping for the answers to finish all those things.

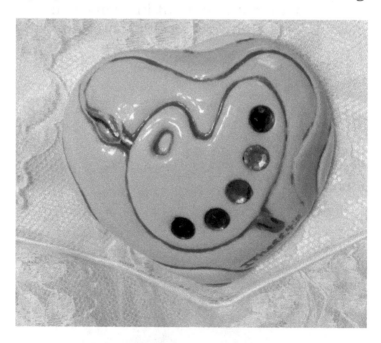

*And that ye study to be quiet, and to do your own
business, and to work with your own hands,*
I Thessalonians 4:11

Paulette Hall

Solitude
January 28, 1995

To be alone with You Lord is what solitude is all about.
To come away with You is where we are founded out.

Because when we are alone with You,
we are nothing in ourselves,

For without You Lord,
we are just an empty shell.

It takes a strength greater than ourselves
to figure this life out,

So, I give my life to You O Lord for
You know what it's all about.

New Beginnings
January 29, 1995

I saw a caterpillar one day,
Inching along with not much to say.

A pitiful creature of greenish yellow,
Not much character the ugly little fellow.

Then one day transformed into a chrysalis so tight,
To be alone and out of sight.

As new life unfolded in that dark solitude,
The sun shone down on that tiny prelude.

The day had arrived, a crack in the casing,
New life merged up, O how amazing!

A wing unwrapped in colors anew,
Another spread out, there were two.

A delight to behold, a new creature in Christ,
Able to fly in freedom with its newfound life.

---

*Therefore if any man be in Christ, he is a new creature: old
things are passed away; behold, all things are become
new.*

II Corinthians 5:17

Paulette Hall

A Fisher of Men
February 6, 1995

As a child Lord, I always loved to go fish'n
with a cane pole, cork, and a worm.

I would wait patiently for the cork to bobble
and the line go tight.

Then with my eyes beholding the tiny jerks on the water;
and the turning of the bobber,
an inexpressible excitement would come over me.

My heart would beat so fast in anticipation of a bite on
the hook. Sometimes I would pull too quickly and miss
the catch, flinging the hook back over my shoulder.

Then there were times when the cork would just
disappear underneath the mirrored glass water,
and the chase was on.

A hard fast catch! And as I remember those fishing
experiences in the natural,
I also hear Your voice as You told

Your disciples, *Follow me, and I will make you
fishers of men.* Matthew 4:19

I like waiting, even though I cannot see underneath the
water. I wait; and in doing what I know to do,
never giving up!

*And let us not be weary in well doing: for in due season we
shall reap, if we faint not.*

Galatians 6:9

103

Shoes of Righteousness
February 6, 1995

Instruments of glory! All praise unto
Your Most Holy Name! Footprints of gold!

A path of righteousness shall be upheld in
the footsteps of my way! You have gone before me!

I shall not be afraid! You have made the shoes that
I must ware. They are a perfect fit for me.

No one else can walk where You have called me to walk.
Only side by side, and hand in hand shall we go.

The path is laid out! Walk ye in it! Finish the race! Mark it
well! Do not look back!

You know every hair on my head!

Paulette Hall

Here I am
February 7, 1995

Here I am Lord at forty-two,
help me to know just what to do.

I am weak and frail, no desires of my own,
To serve You Lord that is why I was born.

Whatever the cost, help me to know,
This life of service I need You to show.

Sometimes I feel that I am stuck in a rut,
Let me not be weighed down with so much stuff.

*But the path of the just is as the shining light, that shineth
more and more unto the perfect day.*

Proverbs 4:18

Lord You are Real

Paulette Hall

Living Waters
February 7, 1995

As I step into Your waters deep,
I hear the sound rush to my feet.

Like a babbling brook, waters flow from Your throne,
You talk and fill, You make me at home.

I hear the sound, Your voice echoes within,
Come away with Me; come away My friend.

The words are good, the words are sweet,
As they turn and swirl about my feet.

A kiss from above,
Your touch is real,

As I stand in awe,
You cover me from head to heel.

A refreshing of a waterfall,
A spray of love comes, I hear Your call.

So, stand in the waters of eternal grace,
When you stand with Me, I give you a place.

Yes, stand with Me, the waters are real,
You are not alone, for you have been sealed.

Ephesians 1:13

Lord You are Real

Fair Maiden
February 17, 1995

A vessel of honor, a vessel of clay,

Formed and fashioned, fair maiden obey.

The Crystal Pitcher
March 24, 1995

You bought a crystal pitcher for a friend you say,
A gift to her for their wedding day.

Intricate cuts were on the surface of the fine glass,
The glass blower must have had a great task.

A beautiful piece was fashioned to hold,
Glistening water, maybe precious flowers
that would heal the soul.

A reflection of the glass blower, the work is unique,
When taken through the fire the picture you see.

It became soft and pliable for a magnificent piece,
No matter how hot there is a sweet release.

Trusting the hand of the Master Designer,
Knowing in His time He is the refiner.

So, let your heart be glad in the beauty you now see,
Rainbows will appear when the Son shines upon thee.

Paulette Hall

I Am There

July 15, 1995

Just over the edge,
over the peak,
I am there.

Awaiting your call,
Awaiting your prayer.

Come to Me.
Talk to Me.
I am there.

Draw nigh to God, and he will draw nigh to you.

James 4:8

Praise Him Intricate Patterns
July 19, 1995

After a loss, and life goes on . . . intricate patterns.

Intricate patterns cut through the sand,
Intricate patterns throughout the land.

Intricate patterns life seems so undone,
Intricate patterns the light shines upon.

Intricate patterns hearts are refined,
Intricate patterns all in God's time.

Intricate patterns one must embrace,
Intricate patterns on an aging face.

Intricate patterns life goes on,
Intricate patterns on and on.

Intricate patterns till the race is run,
Intricate patterns face to the Son.

Intricate patterns soul be at rest,
Intricate patterns to be happy and blessed.

Intricate patterns carved in our hearts,
Intricate patterns never to depart.

Intricate patterns love so divine,
Intricate patterns we were on His mind.

Intricate patterns made at the cross,
Intricate patterns for all the lost.

Intricate patterns why do men fall?

Paulette Hall

Intricate patterns You felt them all.

Intricate patterns sin took its toll,
Intricate patterns made for man's soul.

Intricate patterns in a tiny snowflake,
Intricate patterns You knew our heartache.

Intricate patterns written in time,
Intricate patterns yes love so divine!

Lord You are Real

Patches of You on A Fall Day
October 11, 1995

As the sun sets, I see Your glory.
Your fiery orange colors explode from
ornamental bushes separated by green trees.

A span of green grass touches another explosion of fiery
orange color which connects to a maple tree.

Then another far off tree in the distance
captures patches of orange golden light.

You are glorious! You are shining upon Your creation!
Your heart sings, and smiles with the

Song!

---

*And God saw every thing that he had made, and, behold,
it was very good.
And the evening and the morning were the sixth day.*

Genesis 1:31

*O Lord, how manifold are thy works! in wisdom hast thou
made them all: the earth is full of thy riches.*

Psalm 104:24

*Be thou exalted, O God, above the heavens: let thy glory be
above all the earth.*

Psalm 57:11

Paulette Hall

A Prayer for A Missionary Friend
January 4, 1996

I pray for you that the New Year will be
full of memorable vision!

Kind of like when a new winter's morn has just begun,
and a new fresh snow is upon the ground.

It is early yet, and you get all bundled up to go out into
the snow, excited, and alone.

Then as you walk along you see your breath in the air,
the Lord is with you! With a turn of your head your
footprints are left behind you.

A shrug or two of the shoulders, and a shiver to keep
warm you press forward with the wind brisk
upon your face.

Out of the corner of your eye you see a holly bush covered
with snow like wool. The red berries peak through
with vibrant crimson delight!

As you draw closer, the snow begins to glisten
with radiant sunlight, iridescent jewels.

You reach out and touch the berries; they are wet.
A tear, a smile, all is well!

You have touched a life, and you have touched
My heart says the Lord.

Have a grand New Year for the

Kingdom of God.

113

Searching

January 10, 1996

Is the searching, searching out to things dear and true?
No selfish gain I pray in Thee, to search for things in You.

A treasure chest is open with fragrance and perfume,
A place of peace and warmth found in
Your chamber room.

A closer walk that we may talk, a laugh, a giggle, a sigh,
Life is a search while we are here on this earth of
an adventure of on high.

As we search here, as we search there,
as we search far and wide,

*Thy kingdom come, Thy will be done...*must be our solemn
cry!

Matthew 6:10

Paulette Hall

The Sunset
January 22, 1996

My eyes behold Your beauty, Your masterpiece.

Pinks and blues, grays, and shades.

Your sky is all glorious!

Lord You are Real

Set the Captives Free
January 24, 1996

O Papa! I pray for the lost, the blind, and the lame.

There are those that have eyes, but they cannot see.
There are those that have ears, but they cannot hear.
There are those that have legs, but they cannot walk.

Many are spiritually impaired!
O how I pray for the healing of the spiritually dead.
That You would blow on their dead, dry bones.
That they would come alive in You.

Then they would have eyes to see, ears to hear,
and legs to walk after You O Lord.

Dear Lord, help the lost and undone!
Restore Your people back to life again!

In Jesus name, Amen.

The Spirit of the Lord is upon me, because he hath anointed me to preach the gospel to the poor; he hath sent me to heal the brokenhearted, to preach deliverance to the captives, and recovering of sight to the blind, to set at liberty them that are bruised, To preach the acceptable year of the Lord.

Luke 4:18-19

I am the good shepherd
John 10:7-18

116

Paulette Hall

Well Springs
January 27, 1996

Yahoo! Ribbons and lace! Ribbons and lace!
A celebration is made when face to face.

Bows and flowers, chiffon, and lace,
A celebration of excitement while face to face.

Arms raised high the ribbons flow around,
Head held high Your anointing drips down.

A glorious celebration while dancing before the King,
A newfound Love let hosannas ring!

*Lift up your heads, O ye gates; and be ye lift up, ye
everlasting doors; and the King of glory shall come in. Who
is this King of glory? The Lord strong and mighty, the Lord
mighty in battle.* Psalms 24:7-8

Psalm 150:6 and John 4:23-24

117

Lord You are Real

Wisdom Heirs
January 28, 1996

Whence does wisdom come the sand and sea
should know?
The Creator made wisdom before He formed a soul.

One grain of sand like unto one life washed upon the
shore,
Waves rush in by the mighty hand of
our Master and our Lord.

Years pass by on the shores of time;
heaven and angels sing,
Wisdom appears only in the time spent before the King!

So, when your life seems over,
the time you have been on this earth,
Glean from the time you have spent with
the Master from the day of your new birth.

For it is not in an aged vessel
whence wisdom does appear,
It is in what you do with the time given
while you are actually here.

Because life is as a vapor, here and then it is gone,
Wisdom can only be found
as we become heirs of the throne.

For there is One who lived to be only thirty-three,
He sought His heavenly Father there upon His knees.

If you are older now, and life is not significant,
A prayer from the heart on bended knee
truly will make a difference.

Paulette Hall

Turn to Him, turn to Him, whatever age you are,
Then you will be a wisdom heir, the best decision by far.

He must increase, but I must decrease.

John 3:30

A Sprinkling
February 7, 1996

Splashing up and over the wall,
Can't you just hear the Savior's call.

Rejoice in the King my little one,
Rejoice in Me till your day is done.

For I long to reside in the place of pure rest,
It is your heart I have chosen to be happy and blessed!

*Happy is that people, that is in such a case: yea, happy is
that people, whose God is the Lord.*

Psalm 144:15

Paulette Hall

It Is Beginning to Rain
February 11, 1996

Your rain I hear upon my windowsill,
A cleansing sound laugh O daffodils.

A spray of love from heaven's throne,
I am here my child; you are not alone.

With a tap, tap, tap on the window of your heart,
To moisten your ground O flower spring up!

The thunder is My voice; do not be afraid,
I am the Almighty God Jehovah,
I came to save, save, save!

Job 28:26-28

Fount of Love
June 26, 1996

O fount of Love!
Pour from above.

O fount of wellsprings,
New life He sings.

Keep constant watch in the night,
The water of my soul's delight.

My fount of eternal joy He brings,
Ever so constant, from the Almighty King.

Keep my heart longing with all its might,
Bring forth Your love within my sight.

Living waters pour upon, and flow within,
The cleansing water from the Great I Am!

Paulette Hall

Callous of Love
June 28, 1996

Callous of love I'll labor for You,
No works too hard for Your Kingdom above.

As I look at my hands, they are soft and gentle,
No callous I see across the palm of my hands,

The work is much and a labor of love,
I'll toil for the callous gentle hands divine.

No hardness I see in the touch from above,
A flow of labor with gentleness and love.

Canopy of Love
August 7, 1996

Father, I thank You for Your canopy of love,
Your canopy of strength.

Like an enclosed garden You have called Your own,
To come! To come and dine!

Your dwelling place! Your dwelling place!
Your canopy of strength, Your canopy of love!

You have stretched Your arms out to cover us,
O Canopy of love, garden of rest.
I love You Lord! My dearest soul's search.

You have sought me, and I have found You,

123

Lord You are Real

My love's paradise. My dearest soul's search.

Fresh oil today. Radiant rhapsody.
My dearest soul's search.

Sing, rejoice, be glad with the Song,
My dearest soul's search.

Sing rejoice, be glad with the Song,
My dearest soul's search.

The canopy is in bloom. Sweet fragrance delight.
A song of intimate adoration.

Purified, renewed, washed with heaven's delight.
There is a place of abiding, there is a place.

There is a place of abiding, there is a place.
My dearest soul's search!

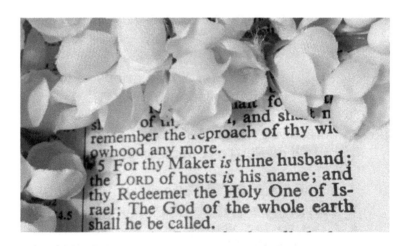

Isaiah 54:5

Paulette Hall

After A Rain
September 1, 1996

Silver drops of rain lay upon a leaf of green,
Teardrops of love fresh upon the scene.

Silent, quiet, still dewdrops of pearls jewel
Your nature wet,
A silver spray of glitter lay upon each branch.

A kiss of love divine, a splash of fragrant fresh,
Your rain a tear of love laying upon each branch.

Wet us with Your love from Your throne of grace,
Rivers of love flowing jewels upon my face.

Teardrops roll pearls upon my cheeks,
An inner love divine, touched by the Prince of Peace.

125

Lord You are Real

Heart of Blue
September 23, 1996

Heart of Blue You were pierced and
bruised for our transgressions.

Royal King clothed in blue,
a cloak of suffering You did bear.

While You walked this earth,
Your sandaled feet touched the dirt.

You endured the suffering and pain Heart of Blue.

Isaiah 9:6 & Isaiah 53

126

Paulette Hall

Winter Underneath the Canopy of Love
January 16, 1999

The tree that once sheltered in spring and summer has
become bare of its covering of green leaves.

Now a fine mist of diamond dust powders the tender herb
beneath the canopy. Winter's frost!
Cool . . . refreshing!

As the morning sun rises, sparkles of dewdrops form,
watering, cleansing, kissing the silent new growth that
awaits Spring's Delight underneath
the canopy of love!

Isaiah 55:10-13

127

Pathway Along the Sand Sea Edge
March 2, 1999

There is a walk along the sand of the sea.
The pathway is narrow. Silent solitude.
Sandaled feet imprint the sand until a white foam crest
wets the indention to be forever remembered in time.

The presence of One mightier than all walks the sand sea
edge. Listening, taking in every sound, every scent.

Sprays of the ocean mist touch,
and whispers of love beckon.
The **S**avior **E**ternal **A**waits!

Psalm 77:19 & Psalm 93:4

Paulette Hall

God's Rainbow
July 30, 2001

Meditation from:
Psalm 145:17
*The Lord is righteous in all his ways, and holy in all his
works.*

II Corinthians 1:20
*For all the promises of God in him are yea, and in him
Amen, unto the glory of God by us.*

Both of these passages confirm our Creator. And when He
created, He was well pleased, and acknowledged His
creation with *yes* and *Amen.*

What God has created; in His beauty and splendor, is a
reflection of who He is to mankind.

Now, when I think about God's promises I think about
His rainbow. This was a promise back to God Himself
reminding Him that He would never destroy man by flood
again.

Now in the beginning there was total darkness.
When God spoke, *Let there be light,* He spoke out Himself
with an array of brilliant colors illuminating all time and
space.

No more darkness. He is Light!

If you have ever studied the human eye, you will discover
a prism of light in the same sequence of the rainbow
which enables our vision; therefore, we have sight.

Lord You are Real

Matthew 6:22 says: *the light of the body is the eye, if therefore thine eye be single, thy whole body shall be full of light.*

When we are single hearted toward Jesus, we are full of His Light, His rainbow.

Now let's look at the rainbow. It speaks of God's promises: It speaks of Him as Creator and His act of creation. It speaks of the Trinity, the God Head.

It speaks of His throne, His dwelling place, and it speaks of His promised return. Our blessed Redeemer.

I want to expound on the beauty and the riches of this significant sign from our Heavenly Father.

The rainbow is Jesus our promised covenant. We also see creation with the seven colors, for God created in six days, and rested on the seventh.

Each color is significant of our relationship to Christ. The seven colors in order are red, orange, yellow, green, blue, indigo, and violet.

This span of color is always in the same order. The Trinity is depicted by the three primary colors.

Red, Yellow, and Blue.

Red is the first color on top of the bow, which represents Jesus, the blood.

Yellow in the middle is significant of God, His Glory, and His Kingdom, our heavenly home. Notice God is always in the center. The yellow is in the center of the rainbow.

The third color blue represents the Holy Spirit.
We think of the blue waters and the blue sky, and how
the Holy Spirit brooded over the waters in the heavenlies.

The mystery of our spiritual birth is revealed by the Holy
Spirit in us through Jesus by washing us clean and
coming to us as a gentle yet mighty rushing wind.

Now let's look at the secondary colors, which appear
in between the three primary colors:

When red and yellow; Jesus and the Father, are blended
together you get orange, the fire of God.

When yellow and blue; The Father and the Holy Spirit, are
blended you get green, new life and eternity.

When you blend blue and red; the Holy Spirit and Jesus,
you get purple, the passion and royalty of God.

Red; the blood, has to run through the entire rainbow
reaching blue; the Holy Spirit, to make the purple tones of
indigo and violet at the bottom of the bow.

This is a beautiful promise of hope; a visual aid our
Heavenly Father has given us,

to see Him as Creator,
to see the Trinity, our God Head, and
to see His promised return and our heavenly home.

Even God's throne is surrounded with the rainbow, His
presence.

Now in Genesis 9:13 God says: *I do set my bow in the
cloud, and it shall be for a token of a covenant between me
and the earth.*

131

Lord You are Real

In Luke 21:27 it is written: *And then shall they see the Son of man coming in a cloud with power and great glory.*

He is the new covenant, and He is the promise. And because He is the promise, all He has told us in His Holy Word are promises for us, His beloved children.

I have to testify that the Lord's promises to us are endless.

He has promised never to leave us or forsake us. He has promised to give us life and give it more abundantly.

He has promised, *I am with you always.* He has promised, *whosoever shall call upon the name of the Lord shall be saved.*

He has promised the Holy Spirit to those who ask. He has promised, *I go to prepare a place for you. And if I go and prepare a place for you,*

I will come again, and receive you unto myself. He has promised He is coming again.

He has promised that His mercies are new every morning and great is His faithfulness.

Again, I must testify that Jesus is the promise of God to us, and we all are created by Him, and for Him.

Nevertheless, it is our choice to follow Him. He is a gentleman, and patiently awaits our hearts cry.

We all are fearfully and wonderfully made. Yes and Amen!

Paulette Hall

And we who are followers of Jesus Christ are carriers of His bow inside of us.

So color your world with His Love.

I Corinthians 13:13

God Moments (true story)
April 22, 2002

A few weeks prior to April 22nd, for some strange
unknown reason my thoughts were bombarded with
questions of if I was really saved or not.
Days went by with these thoughts.

Then the morning of April 22nd; as I was getting out of
my car to go to work, I heard in the distance a voice, like
someone was talking on a transistor radio.
It seemed to get louder and louder.

I found myself leaning forward to see where the blaring
sound was coming from. Then, suddenly, the voice arced
onto the power lines above me.

It was like amplified speakers in the heavens.
I was totally surrounded by a loud voice,

"Don't worry about your salvation, God will take care of
it." Needless to say, I was astounded at what I had heard.

There were two other employees walking into the building
the same time as I was. So, I asked "Did you hear that?"

They both responded yes, but did not understand
what was said. I replied, "I did."

They asked what I had heard. I told them both, and one
asked me to repeat it. So, I did.

Then one of them said, "Well, every knee will bow."
Then I repeated,

"Don't worry about your salvation,

Paulette Hall

God will take care of it!"
We all smiled as we entered together.

As we parted our ways, I walked to my office so full
of excitement of that encounter.

The first person I came in contact with got splashed on.
I just had to tell someone.

They teared up as I shared what I had experienced.

Then I realized that those earlier thoughts of doubt
about my salvation were from the enemy.
That rascal is such a liar!

---

*The thief cometh not, but for to steal, and to kill, and to
destroy. I am come that they might have life, and that they
might have it more abundantly.*

John 10:10

Your Word
February 22, 2009

Your Word, treasures from above,
Transforms my heart with Your divine love.

May Your treasured threads of silver, and gold,
Intertwine the fiber of my very soul.

135

*The Lord on high is mightier than the noise
of many waters,
yea, than the mighty waves of the sea.*

Psalm 93:4

John's Pass, Tampa Florida 1994

Paulette Hall

John's Pass 1994
June 12, 2018

My Dad and I got into a discussion
of creation versus evolution.

He did not want to talk about it anymore, I guess because
I was pretty firm about creation.

I had never really been so outspoken to my Dad than
that day. I felt bad about it later, because
I did not want to dishonor him in any way.

I began praying sincerely for him then, and for many days
forward. I knew Dad had accepted Christ when he was a
young man, so I wasn't concerned about his salvation,
only the conflict between creation and evolution.

About a week later he and mom went to Tampa, Florida.
After they returned home,
my dad said he had something for me from God.

I looked on the coffee table where he pointed and there
was a brown bag with seven seashells enclosed.
Dad proceeded to tell me that as he was cast fishing at
John's Pass early one morning something rolled in and
bumped up against his foot.

He said he reached down and picked up a shell, and
before throwing it back into the ocean,
he said, "This must be for Paulette."
So, he put it in his pocket.

Then another bump, and another, and another, and
another, and another, and another.

There were seven seashells that had rolled up to

Lord You are Real

Dad's feet. As I studied the shells, I could see that they resembled our family. Each shell was in descending order in size. The first two were similar in kind, two conch shells representing Mom and Dad. One thin and tall: Dad, the other short, worn, and bleached out by the salt water with a few barnacles attached: Mom.

The next five shells represented the five children. Three boys, and two girls.

The first two were similar in kind; two boys, then the next two were similar in kind except different from the first two; two girls, and the last shell was similar in kind as the first two but smaller in size, one more boy.

Also, because there were seven shells, it made me think of creation and how God rested on the seventh day.

They also reminded me of the rainbow with its seven bows of color, and how the rainbow represents the everlasting covenant which God set in place as a reminder to Himself that He would never destroy the earth by flood again. Genesis 9:13-16

Jesus; the everlasting covenant, will return in the clouds. Revelation 1:7

It was no coincidence when those seven seashells rolled in at my Dad's feet.

They spoke of creation and our family, and even Dad acknowledged that they were from God.

Before Mom and Dad had returned home from their trip, I had a unique dream connecting me to my Dad and to God. I was at the ocean edge looking into the glistening water, and lo to my surprise,

I saw fragments of broken pottery, whose once sharp
edges now had been smoothed by the constant ocean
waves. Each piece; though varied in sizes, were
hand-painted scenes of Jesus with a saxophone in His
arms.

I gathered many from the glistening water. (Later, I
questioned why a saxophone? Then I realized that in real
life my dad loved this musical instrument.
So God had placed it in my dream with Jesus on those
hand-painted pottery pieces that I had found at the
oceans edge. God was letting me know not to be worried
about my dad, and that Jesus is taking good care of him.)

Then my dream changed to a different scene. I had my
beautiful treasures in hand standing at an elevator door.

I laid those precious jewels inside and turned for a
moment when the elevator door closed, and those
treasures headed upward.

I awoke.

Oh my! I was so disappointed that my findings
at the sand sea edge were gone.

Then the Spirit of the Lord; with His still small voice,
comforted my soul and said,

"Do not worry my child your treasures are in
heaven with Me".

Matthew 6:19-21

It is Raining Outside
June 25, 2018

Thank You for this beautiful rain! The sound is so refreshing so clean and pure. The smell is sweet.

I hear Your thunder in the background. I am reminded of Isaiah 55:8-13

How beautiful is Your Word! I see new lime-green growth at the tips of an oak branch against the backdrop of a darker hue of green among the older foliage of leaves. So pretty. It makes me smile inside.

Everything is washed and bathed with Your heavenly water. A sweet breeze blows across my face touching my cheeks.

My sight captures a few strands of hair flowing across my brow in movement with the breeze. Everything is still and quiet . . . a long roll of thunder in the distance breaks the silence.

Your beauty is all around! Sweet caresses from Your throne of grace. My senses are aware, alert!

My sight captures a bird in flight. My ear hears sounds of Your outdoors. I feel Your breeze, and I smell Your fragrant air! Ahhh!

You are raining outside, and You are reigning within my heart!

Paulette Hall

Canopy of Three Trees
August 9, 2018

Sitting outside, the world around me,
Mine eye does see a canopy of three trees.

With cars zooming by, I sense Your peace and ease,
Because of those three trees standing before me.

Then I look up high above those three trees,
In the far distance a soaring bird away in the breeze.

My soul is wanting, and now telling me,
Fly high my child, like unto the bird you see.

For My Presence is always, and forever before thee,
Remember this visual canopy of these three trees.

Remember this visual canopy of these three trees,
The Father, the Son, the Holy Spirit speaking to thee.

Ode to an Oyster Strands of Pearls
September 26, 2018

When the grit and grime of this world comes in upon us, it irritates and is uncomfortable to our soul.

Like unto an oyster when a particle of sand enters the soft muscle tissue, it will secrete a milky substance that covers the grain of sand until a smooth pebble is formed.

It no longer irritates the tender insides of the oyster, and the tiny grit of sand has become a pearl.

That is what the Holy Spirit will do for us humans when things irritate our inward being.

He; the Holy Spirit, will cover that area with the milk of God's Word; Jesus, until that uncomfortable particle has become a Precious Pearl.

Strands of pearls for all will see, the hidden treasures made within thee.

But seek ye first the kingdom of God, and his righteousness; and all these things shall be added unto you.

Matthew 6:33

Paulette Hall

Arduous Times
November 13, 2018

Lord the walk has been arduous at times.

I am weepy today, but I know You are with me!

Help me to finish the race.
To finish the work
You have called me to.

To be a soul winner . . .
that many will see, and come to know
You in all Your glory and grace.

Christ shall be magnified! Amen.

*And Jesus said unto them, I am the bread of life: he that
cometh to me shall never hunger; and he that believeth on
me shall never thirst.*
John 6:35

Lord You are Real

It Is Raining
February 11, 2019

There is just something about the rain.

Pure clear droplets coming down from the heavens,
watering the ground and all the green herbs of the field.

A refreshing! I feel like I am playing in the rain.
Like a little child, splashing, laughing, twirling with head
held back, face up toward the sky, feeling the gentle
spattering of Your wet kisses on my cheeks and forehead.

I taste the sweet drops in my mouth.
With arms outstretched, the palms of my hands feel
Your touch of love!

Your rain is like unto piano keys suspended in the air; my
fingers are playing each drop.
I can hear Your melody!
Your Song of Love!

With legs marching forward, and with each step taken,
the soles of my feet plunge into the silver glassed puddles
of collected wet moisture. The water around those
footprints spurts upward, and outward. A splash of
gladness, joy, and peace reeling through my heart and
soul.

A thrill of washing. A newness awakens
my heart to embrace all that You have.

I am Your child. Your little girl. Your daughter. May
I splash on others as You have splashed on me.

Thank You, my Reigning King. Thank You for the rain!
My Reigning King!

144

Paulette Hall

Poured Out
February 23, 2019

To be a vintage wine bottle today Heavenly Father.
Ready to be poured out for You Lord.

You have refined, mellowed, sweetened,
and prepared it for this hour and for Your glory.

*Thou preparest a table before me in the presence of mine
enemies: thou anointest my head with oil; my cup runneth
over. Surely goodness and mercy shall follow me all the
days of my life: and I will dwell in the house of the Lord for
ever.*
Psalm 23:5-6

May the ears that hear receive a fresh drink from Your
table. And now; from this bottle of wine You have
prepared, may the hearers taste and see that
The Lord, He is good.

You are the crimson flow; You are the New Wine. It is a
refreshing that will heal, repair, renew, and fill each
heart. For You are the One who heals, the One who
repairs, the One who renews, and the One who fills.

You are He! And I am so thankful! Bless Your Holy Name!
Your name shall be magnified forever.
Amen

---

*How beautiful upon the mountains are the feet of him that
bringeth good tidings, that publisheth peace; that bringeth
good tidings of good, that publisheth salvation; that saith
unto Zion, Thy God reigneth!*
Isaiah 52:7

Taken by Your Beauty
February 28, 2019

It is raining today.
I am so taken with You Lord.
I am taken with You.

As I am outside viewing Your nature wet,
I see crystal clear drops hanging on the
bare brittle winter branches.

The beauty of Your touch caresses Your creation. The
swollen droplets cling like heavenly jewels. . . thousands.
They glisten with an iridescent sparkle.

I took a few close-up pictures, but a picture cannot
capture Your intricate beauty.

I can hardly take it all in myself. My eyes begin to well up.
Teardrops; warm, began to roll down my cheeks.
You are all glorious! You alone are Awesome!

I feel Your watering of love within my own heart.
An inexpressible print of devotion overflows.

I am reminded of You saying, *I am the vine, and ye are the
branches: He that abideth in me, and I in him, the same
bringeth forth much fruit: for without me ye can do nothing.*

John 15:5

Wet us with Your love.
Rain on Your people.
Water us with Your words.

Paulette Hall

It soon will be spring, and soon new growth.
May we, Your people bear much fruit for
Your Kingdom. Amen.

Oasis
May 13, 2019

Thank You for the desert times!
The desert place is dry, cracked, and parched.

To thirst after You, and You alone.
You are the springs of water in the desert.

Fresh cool water, You are shelter from the scorching sun.
There we find our Oasis. You are our Oasis.

Unbroken Communion
Intimacy of The Heart
May 27, 2019

May we Your people commune with You.

May we look above our circumstance to You.

May we see Your hand of mercy holding us.

May we hear Your voice of love speaking to our hearts.

May we desire unbroken communion with You,
as You do with us.

May we acknowledge that we desperately need You.

May we surrender our lives to You.

May we abide under the shadow of Your wings.

May intimacy of the heart never end. Amen.

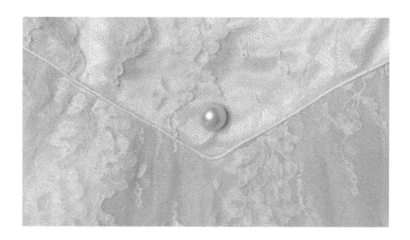

Paulette Hall

Our Mom
December 14, 2019

She so loved her family, friends, and never met a
stranger. She was giving, talented and creative.

She was fun, adventurous, an amazing cook, witty,
loved by many, and a beautiful soul!

One thing my mom etched in my memory as a child
was her respect for God's word.

I remember many times, whenever the Bible slipped from
her hand, she would pick it up and kiss it.

So later, when I turned my life over to the Lord and began
to grow in His word, that precious memory of mom's kiss
surfaced as a true blessing to my heart.

I realized what a beautiful book
God had left His children, and it
is so worthy of kisses.

Thank You, Heavenly Father, for
the gift of our precious mom
Violet, and the gift of Your
precious Word!
Kiss, Kiss

O Death Where is Thy Sting?
March 9, 2020

Grandpa and I ventured out one day to go a fish'n.
The wooden boat tottered back and forth
as we stepped in.

With paddle in his hand, the tiny boat for two
glided out into the pond.
It was a very hot summer's day.

As the boat settled in place, and the anchor was dropped,
Grandpa reached his hand into the wire-bait-basket
for a fat cricket.

With my head turned aside, I never could watch him
bait the hook.
He then flipped the leaded line into the water.

The cork bobber placed the position for the catch beneath
and rested so still on the water's surface.
Rings encircled the thin nylon line.

Minding my own business while waiting and watching the
ripples of bubbles merge to the top,
an O black wasp landed on my knee. Ouch!
A burning stinger left behind.

Grandpa took out of his pocket an old crumpled pack of
loose tobacco. With not a word spoken he pinched
off a piece and popped it in his mouth.

Before I knew it, he had daubed it on top of my knee
where the stinger had been embedded.
His aged hand wiping away my tears, with a gentle smile,
and a nod of his head he carefully returned to
his seat in the rocking wooden boat.

150

After a few minutes, the fiery pain had subsided, and
when the saliva moistened patch of
crushed-brown leaves were removed, the stinger was gone
too. What a surprise!

As I am much older now, I often look back on that hot
summer's day with grandpa.
Remembering how that stinger was removed.

O death, where is thy sting? O grave, where is thy victory?

*The sting of death is sin; and the strength of sin is the law.
But thanks be to God, which giveth us the victory through
our Lord Jesus Christ.*

*Therefore, my beloved brethren, be ye steadfast,
unmovable, always abounding in the work of the Lord,
forasmuch as ye know that your labour is not in vain in the
Lord.*

I Corinthians 15:55-58, John 1:17 & 14:21

The Gathering of Seashells
April 6, 2020

The gathering of seashells,
On a sandy beach.
The gathering of seashells,
Never beyond His reach.

The gathering of seashells,
Washed in by ocean waves.
The gathering of seashells,
His life He gave.

The gathering of seashells,
Each one different and unique.
The gathering of seashells,
Behold His beauty on each piece.

The gathering of seashells,
The time has come.
The gathering of seashells,
Of His beloved chosen ones.

Blessed be the Lord God of Israel; for he hath visited and redeemed his people.

Luke 1:68

And I will give them one heart, and I will put a new spirit within you; and I will take the stony heart out of their flesh, and will give them an heart of flesh: That they may walk in my statutes, and keep mine ordinances, and do them: and they shall be my people, and I will be their God.

Ezekiel 11:19-20

Paulette Hall

Beauty Rests in The Power of The Cross
April 9, 2020

Amid the roses Beauty Rests,
Sight unseen, foretold.
It is the scent of Heaven's Best,
That fills the heart and soul.

A purple rose upon the cross,
His Passion from God's own hand.
A mighty love amongst the thorns,
The Deliverer of sinful man.

Hearts forgiven, lives transformed,
The Purple Rose arisen.
New life we find when we look on high,
For the Passion God has given.

Seek first Thy Kingdom from heaven above,
Where Peace, and Love is found.
The Word, My Son, His life foretold,
Heaven's Power shall forever abound.

Paulette Hall

I am the rose of Sharon,
and the lily of the valleys.
As the lily among thorns,
so is my love among the daughters.

Song of Solomon 2:1

For the preaching of the cross is to them
that perish foolishness;
but unto us which are saved
it is the power of God.

I Corinthians 1:18

God
So
Loves
You

John 3:16

Invitation

Please Come

A shower's being hosted
for a lovely bride-to-be.
Sure, hope you can be there
to help the day go perfectly.

For: **You (whosoever will)**
Revelation 22:17

Date: **unknown** Time: **unknown**
Matthew 25:13

Place: **The Holy City, The New Jerusalem**
Revelation 21:2

Given by: **The Lord God Almighty**
Revelation 19:6-9

RSVP: **Choose you this day whom
You will serve**
Joshua 24:15

And the Spirit and the bride say, Come.
Revelation 22:17

But whosoever drinketh of the water that I shall give hi[m]

shall never thirst;

but the water that I shall give him

shall be in him a well of water

springing up into everlasting life.

John 4:14

Paulette Hall

About the Author

Paulette Hall is an inspirational writer and artist. She has an AA degree from Kennesaw State University in Kennesaw, Georgia.

In 1987 Paulette hand carved and painted God's word on clay hearts in a visual form creating The Living Hearts Collection. She began her art ministry of visual evangelism in 1989.

In addition to her art ministry; which has been viewed in the work place, colleges (like KSU and Reinhardt University in Waleska, Georgia), libraries, book stores, churches, government buildings, assisted living centers, art exhibits, and art galleries, her visual displays from1989-2000 at the Apparel Mart, and the World Congress Center for the Festival Of Trees, have been viewed by an innumerable list of patrons; as well as, many men, women, and children from all walks of life.

The display themes for the Festival Of Trees are as follows:

1.) The Living Christmas Tree, 1989 (tree displayed with The Livings Hearts Collection ©1987)

2.) Love Grew Where The Blood Fell, 1990 (seven foot white tree), Love Crucified A Rose (wreath)

3.) Golden Jubilee, 1991 (wreath with gold trumpets, cross, yellow rose and yellow bows)

4.) The Scarlet Thread of Redemption, 1992 (wreath depicting the lineage of Jesus, and poem)

5.) Rhapsody In Bloom, 1993 (musical wall art with grape clusters, roses, cross, and poem)

6.) Follow Me, 1994 (six foot cross dressed with fishnet, names of God, including the twelve tribes of Israel)

7.) Tree Of Life, 1995 (six foot cross, draped with red velvet fabric, and crown of thorns)

8.) Crown Him Lord Of All, 1996 (round seven foot display of five handmade crowns from the Bible plus crown of thorns)

9.) The King Is Coming, 1997 (six foot cross dressed with handwoven Priestly Garments)

10.) The Apple Of Thine Eye, 1998 (six foot cross draped with crushed red velvet, & crown of thorns)

11.) Suffer The Little Children To Come Unto Me, 1999 (wreath, with roses and picture of children with Jesus)

12.) The Wedding Feast Awaits You, 2000 (honeycomb shaped gazebo with cross dressed as Bridegroom in center)

Paulette has worked in business administration for forty years and retired in 2018 from Wellstar Health System. She now continues in ministry through sharing her creativity with others.

In her leisure time she enjoys gardening, walking, reading, fishing, and spending time with family and friends.

CPSIA information can be obtained
at www.ICGtesting.com
Printed in the USA
FSHW021339111020
74614FS